Classic Pub Jokes

ISBN: 1 84161 216 2

This edition first published by Ravette Publishing in 2004.

Printed and bound in Malaysia
for Ravette Publishing Limited
Unit 3, Tristar Centre, Star Road, Partridge Green,
West Sussex RH13 8RA
United Kingdom

Classic Pub Jokes

Introduction

There is nothing better than a good dose of humour to brighten any day. Okay, well, we know food and shelter and health and love and world peace all have their places, but they don't exactly make you laugh in any sidesplitting way. They don't tickle your funny bone like a good joke might. In fact, it would be a strange world without laughter, and everyone would go about with long, serious faces, wondering when someone was going to invent humour.

All in all the world would be a pretty glum place—unlike it is today. But it would be wrong to believe that just because laughter has been with us for quite a long time now, it will just always be here. Even now, as you read these very words, forces are at work to rid the world of laughter. Which could be a serious loss! But despair not! Here is a collection of all the best pub jokes, just the thing to start you on the road to saving the world from becoming too serious. Read them and laugh to yourself, or memorise them and seek a new line of work as a stand-up pub comedian. The choice is yours, just don't blame us if it doesn't work out.

A dog with one leg walks into a western bar and says to the bartender,
'I'm looking for the man who shot my paw...!'

A man walks into a bar with a steering wheel in his underpants.
'Is that painful?' the barman asks.
'It's driving me nuts!' the man replies.

A brain went into a pub and says, 'Pint of lager, please.'
'Sorry mate, you're already out of your head,' the barman replies.

Two drunks are in a pub sitting at the bar, staring into their drinks.
One gets a curious look on his face and asks, 'Hey, Pete, have you ever seen an ice cube with a hole in it before?'
'Yep. I been married to one for fifteen years.'

A mushroom walks into a bar, sits down and orders a drink. The bartender says, 'I'm afraid we don't serve mushrooms here.'
'Why not? I'm a fun guy!'

The Best Pub:

An Irishman, an Italian, and a Polish guy are in a bar. They are having a good time and all agree that the bar is a nice place.

Then the Irishman says, 'Aye, this is a nice bar, but where I come from, back in Dublin, there's a better one. At MacDougal's, you buy a drink, you buy another drink, and MacDougal himself will buy your third drink!' The others agree that sounds like a nice place.

Then the Italian says, 'Yeah, that's a nice bar, but where I come from, there's a better one. Over in Brooklyn, there's this place, Vinny's. At Vinny's, you buy a drink, Vinny buys you a drink. You buy anudda drink, Vinny buys you anudda drink.' Everyone agrees that sounds like a great bar.

Then the Polish guy says, 'You think that's great? Where I come from, there's this place called Warshowski's. At Warshowski's, they buy you your first drink, they buy you your second drink, they buy you your third drink, and then, they take you in the back and get you laid!'

'Wow!' say the other two. 'That's fantastic! Do you go there often?'

'No,' replies the Polish guy, 'but my wife does.'

A man walks into a bar—he sits down and orders a drink. The barman gives him his drink, accompanied by a bowl of peanuts. To his surprise, a voice comes from the peanut bowl. 'You look great tonight!' it said, 'You really look fantastic... and that aftershave is just wonderful!'

The man is obviously a little confused, but tries to ignore it. Realising he has no cigarettes he wanders over to the cigarette machine. After inserting his money, another voice emits from the machine.

'You're a TOTAL WANKER... My God you STINK... Do you know, you're almost AS UGLY AS YOUR MOTHER!'

By now, the man is extremely perplexed. He turns to the barman for an explanation. 'Ah yes sir,' the barman responds, 'The peanuts are complimentary, but the cigarette machine is out of order.'

* * * * *

A neutron goes into a bar and asks the barman, 'How much for a beer?'

'For you, no charge,' the barman replies.

A guy walks into a bar and sits down. He starts dialling numbers... like a telephone... on his hand and talking into his hand.

The bartender walks over and tells him this is a very tough neighbourhood and he doesn't need any trouble here.

The guy says, 'You don't understand. I'm very hi-tech. I had a phone installed in my hand because I was tired of carrying the cellular.'

The bartender says 'Prove it.'

The guy dials up a number and hands his hand to the bartender. The bartender talks into the hand and carries on a conversation. 'That's incredible,' says the bartender. 'I would never have believed it!'

'Yeah,' said the guy, 'I can keep in touch with my broker, my wife, you name it. By the way, where is the men's room?' The bartender directs him to the men's room. The guy goes in and 5, 10, 20 minutes go by and he doesn't return.

Fearing the worst given the neighbourhood, the bartender goes into the men's room. There is the guy spread-eagle on the wall. His pants are pulled down and he has a roll of toilet paper up his butt.

'Oh my god!' said the bartender. 'Did they rob you? Are you hurt?'

The guy turns and says: 'No, I'm ok. I'm just waiting for a fax.'

* * * * *

An Indian walks into a bar with a bag in one hand and a cat in the other. He sits down at the bar and orders a whiskey, throws the bag in the corner, pulls out his gun and shoots the bag, causing shit to fly out of the bag. He then starts to eat the cat, slamming the whiskey afterwards.

The dumbfounded bartender asks 'What the hell are you doing?!'

The Indian replies 'Me want to be like white man—drink whiskey eat pussy and shoot the shit.'

* * * * *

A sandwich goes into a pub, walks up to the barman, and says, 'Pint of lager please.'

'Sorry mate,' says the barman, 'we don't serve food in here.'

A man was sitting in the bar when he noticed another patron a few stools away. The guy had a body like Charles Atlas, but his head was the size of a thimble.

The first man said, 'Please excuse me for staring, but I can't help but be curious as to why your body is so well developed, but your head is so small?'

The man said, 'Buy me a drink and I'll tell you.' The drink was ordered and the story began. 'I was in the navy and my ship was sunk by a torpedo. I was the only survivor and I managed to make it to a deserted island a few miles away. I had been there for several months and was sitting on the beach one day waiting for a bird or fish to come by so I would have something to eat. Then looking up I saw a beautiful mermaid sunning on a nearby rock. She swam over to me and informed me that she was a magical mermaid and could grant me three wishes.

'Great I said. I'd like to be rescued.' She slapped the water with her tail and a ship appeared, sailing straight for my island.

Next I asked for a body like Charles Atlas. Another slap of the tail and here it is.

Then, noticing how beautiful she was and all my other wishes fulfilled I asked if I could make love to her. She said that it just wouldn't work, her being half fish and all, so I said 'well, okay, if we can't have sex, can you just give me a little head then?"

* * * * *

The Obliging Doorman:

Leaving a plush night club one evening, a miserly gentleman walked past the doorman without tipping him. Never the less, the doorman helped the man into a taxi with a flourish and said pleasantly. 'By the way, in case you happen to lose your wallet on the way home, Sir, just remember that you didn't pull it out here.'

* * * * *

A lady goes into a bar with her goose. Then the bartender comes up to her and says, 'Why did you have to bring the pig in with you?'

Then the lady answered, 'Excuse me, I think this is a goose.'

And the bartender says, 'Excuse me, I was talking to the goose.'

Every night after dinner, Merle took off for the local watering hole. He would spend the whole evening there and always arrive home, quite inebriated, around midnight each night.

He usually had trouble getting his key to fit the keyhole and couldn't get the door open. And every time this happened, his wife would go to the door and let him in. Then she would proceed to yell and scream at him, for his constant nights out and always coming home in a drunken state. But Merle just continued his nightly routine.

One day, the wife was talking to a friend about her husband's behavior and was particularly distraught by it all.

The friend listened and said, 'Why don't you treat him a little differently when he comes home? Instead of berating him, why don't you give him some loving words and welcome him home with a kiss? Then he might change his ways.'

The wife thought that this might be a good idea.

That night, Merle took off again after dinner. And at about midnight, he arrived home in his usual condition.

His wife heard him at the door. She quickly opened it and let Merle in.

Instead of berating him as she had always done, this time she took his arm and led him into the living room. She sat Merle down in an easy chair, put his feet up on the ottoman and took his shoes off. Then she went behind him and started to cuddle him a little. After a little while, she said to Merle, 'It's pretty late, dear. I think we had better go upstairs to bed now, don't you think?'

At that, in his inebriated state he replied, 'I guess we might as well. I'll get in trouble when I get home anyway!'

* * * * *

Two drunks are at a bar, drinking up a storm.

One drunk says to the other drunk, 'Did you sleep with my wife last night?'

To which the other drunk replies, 'Not a wink.'

A policeman pulls over a driver for swerving in and out of lanes on the highway. He tells the guy to blow a breath into a breathalyzer.

'I can't do that, officer.'

'Why not?'

'Because I'm an asthmatic. I could get an asthma attack if I blow into that tube.'

'Okay, we'll just get a urine sample down at the station.'

'Can't do that either, officer.'

'Why not?'

'Because I'm a diabetic. I could get low blood sugar if I pee in a cup.'

'Alright, we could get a blood sample.'

'Can't do that either, officer.'

'Why not?'

'Because I'm a hemophiliac. If I give blood I could die.'

'Fine then, just walk this white line.'

'Can't do that either, officer.'

'Why not?'

'Because I'm drunk.'

A man is in bed with his wife when there is a knock on the door. He rolls over and looks at his clock—it's half-past three in the morning.

'I'm not getting out of bed at this time', he thinks, and rolls over. Then, a louder knock follows. 'Aren't you going to answer that?' says his wife. So, he drags himself out of bed and goes downstairs.

He opens the door and there is man standing at the door. It didn't take the homeowner long to realise the man was drunk. 'Hi there,' slurs the stranger, 'Can you give me a push?'

'No. Get lost, it's half past three. I was in bed,' says the man and slams the door.

He goes back up to bed and tells his wife what happened and she says 'Dave, that wasn't very nice of you.

Remember that night we broke down in the pouring rain on the way to pick the kids up from the baby-sitter and you had to knock on that man's door to get us started again? What would have happened if he'd told us to get lost?'

'But the guy was drunk,' says the husband.

'It doesn't matter,' says the wife. 'He needs our help and it would be the Christian thing to help him.'

So the husband gets out of bed again, gets dressed and goes downstairs. He opens the door and, not being able to see the stranger anywhere he shouts: 'Hey, do you still want a push?' and he hears a voice cry out 'Yeah please.'

So, still being unable to see the stranger, he shouts: 'Where are you?'

And the stranger replies: 'I'm over here, on your swingset.

* * * * *

A guy goes into a bar, orders twelve shots and starts drinking them as fast as he can.

The bartender says, 'Dang, why are you drinking so fast?'

The guy says, 'You would be drinking fast if you had what I had.'

The bartender says, 'What do you have?'

The guy says, 'Seventy-five cents.'

A man who smelled like a distillery flopped down on a subway seat next to a priest. The man's tie was stained, his face was plastered with red lipstick, and a half-empty bottle of gin was sticking out of his torn coat pocket.

He opened his newspaper and began reading. After a few minutes, the disheveled guy turned to the priest and asked, 'Say, Father, what causes arthritis?'

'Mister, it's caused by loose living, being with cheap women, too much alcohol and a contempt for your fellow man!'

'Well, I'll be damned!' the drunk muttered, returning to his paper.

The priest, thinking about what he had said, nudged the man and apologized. 'I'm very sorry, I shouldn't have been so unpleasant about it. Tell me, how long have you had arthritis?'

'I don't have it, Father—I was just reading here that the Pope does!'

The FDA is considering additional warnings on beer and alcohol bottles, such as:

WARNING: consumption of alcohol may make you think you are whispering when you are not.

WARNING: consumption of alcohol is a major factor in dancing like an idiot.

WARNING: consumption of alcohol may cause you to tell the same boring story over and over again until your friends want to SMASH YOUR HEAD IN.

WARNING: consumption of alcohol may cause you to thay shings like thish.

WARNING: consumption of alcohol may lead you to believe that ex-lovers are really dying for you to telephone them at four in the morning.

WARNING: consumption of alcohol may leave you wondering what the hell happened to your pants.

WARNING: consumption of alcohol may cause you to roll over in the morning and see something really scary (whose species and/or name you can't remember).

WARNING: consumption of alcohol is the leading cause of inexplicable rug burns on the forehead.

WARNING: consumption of alcohol may create the illusion that you are tougher, more handsome and smarter than some really, really big guy named Thor.

WARNING: consumption of alcohol may lead you to believe you are invisible.

WARNING: consumption of alcohol may lead you to think people are laughing WITH you.

WARNING: Consumption of alcohol may cause an disruption in the space-time continuum, whereby small (and sometimes large) gaps of time may seem to 'disappear'.

WARNING: Consumption of alcohol may actually CAUSE pregnancy.

* * * * *

Q: How can you tell the difference between Beer Nuts and Deer Nuts?

A: The Beer Nuts are about a dollar fifty and the Deer Nuts are under a Buck.

What I done in Texas:

A cowboy rode into town and stopped at a saloon for a drink. Unfortunately, the locals always had a habit of picking on strangers. When he finished his drink, he found his horse had been stolen.

He went back into the bar, handily flipped his gun into the air, caught it above his head without even looking and fired a shot into the ceiling.

'Which one of you sidewinders stole my horse?' he yelled forcefully.

No one answered.

'All right, I'm gonna have another beer, and if my horse ain't back outside by the time I finish, I'm gonna do what I dun in Texas! And I don't like to have to do this.

Some of the locals shifted restlessly. The man, true to his word, had another beer, walked outside, and his horse has been returned to the post.

He saddled up and started to ride out of town. The bartender wandered out of the bar and asked, 'Say partner, before you go, what happened in Texas?'

The cowboy turned back and said, 'I had to walk home.'

Everything's Big

There once was a blind man who decided to visit Texas. When he got onto the plane, he felt the seats and said, 'Wow, these seats are big!'

The person next to him answered, 'Everything is big in Texas.'

When he finally arrived in Texas, he decided to visit a bar. Upon arriving in the bar, he ordered a beer and got a mug placed between his hands.

He exclaimed, 'Wow these mugs are big!'

The bartender replied, 'Everything is big in Texas.'

After a couple of beers, the blind man asked the bartender where the bathroom was located. The bartender replied, 'Second door to the right.'

The blind man headed for the bathroom, but accidentally tripped and skipped the second door. Instead, he entered the third door, which lead to the swimming pool and fell in by accident.

Scared to death, the blind man started shouting, 'Don't flush, don't flush!'

Cut Off

A man walks in the front door of a bar. He is obviously drunk, and staggers up to the bar, seats himself on a stool and with a belch, asks the bartender for a drink.

The bartender politely informs the man it appears that he has already had plenty to drink, he could not be served additional liquor at this bar, and could a cab be called for him?

The drunk is briefly surprised, then softly scoffs, grumbles, climbs down off the bar stool and staggers out the front door.

A few minutes later, the same drunk stumbles in the side door of the bar. He wobbles up to the bar and hollers for a drink. The bartender comes over and, still politely—but more firmly, refuses service to the man due to his inebriation, and again offers to call a cab.

The drunk looks at the bartender for a moment angrily, curses, and shows himself out the side door, all the while grumbling and shaking his head.

A few minutes later, the same drunk bursts in through the back door of the bar. He plops himself up on a bar stool, gathers his wits and belligerently orders a drink.

The bartender comes over and emphatically reminds the man that he is clearly drunk, will be served no drinks, and either a cab or the police will be called immediately.

The surprised drunk looks at the bartender, and in hopeless anguish, cries, 'Man! How many bars do you work at?'

* * * * *

Piece of string walks into the bar. 'Are you a piece of string?' asks the barman.

'Yes,' replies the piece of string.

'Sorry mate, you'll have to leave, we don't serve your kind here.'

The piece of string leaves, disappointed. The next day he ties a knot in his middle, ruffles up one end of himself, and goes back in.

'Oi! I told you yesterday to get out, you're that piece of string aren't you?'

'No, I'm afraid not.'

Smart Thinking

A very shy guy goes into a bar and sees a beautiful woman sitting at the counter. After an hour of gathering up his courage he finally goes over to her and asks, tentatively, 'Um, would you mind if I chatted with you for a while?'

She responds by yelling, at the top of her lungs, 'No, I won't sleep with you tonight!'

Everyone in the bar is now staring at them.

Naturally, the guy is hopelessly and completely embarrassed and he slinks back to his table.

After a few minutes, the woman walks over to him and apologizes.

She smiles at him and says, 'I'm sorry if I embarrassed you. You see, I'm a graduate student in psychology and I'm studying how people respond to embarrassing situations.'

To which he responds, at the top of his lungs, 'What do you mean $200?'

Two alcoholics are skint and desperate for a beer when one of them comes up with a brilliant idea for getting some free booze.

'I've got 20p left says John, I'll go and buy a sausage and I'll stick it in your fly before we go into the pub, trust me it can't fail.'

So into the pub they go and order 2 doubles which they down in one. When the barman asks for the money, John drops to his knees and starts to suck on the sausage sticking out of his mates trousers.

'You dirty bastards,' screams the barman and throws them out.

The two men continue all day using the same trick, until they are legless.

'My knees are killing me with all that kneeling down,' says John.

'That's nothing' says his mate.'I lost the sausage at the second pub.'

A new guy in town walks into a bar and reads a sign that hangs over the bar.

FREE BEER FOR THE PERSON WHO CAN PASS OUR TEST!

So the guy asks the bartender what the test is. The Bartender replies 'Well, first you have to drink that whole gallon of pepper tequila, the whole thing at once and you can't make a face while doing it. Second, there's a 'gator out back with a sore tooth...you have to remove it with your bare hands. Third, there's a woman up-stairs who's never had an orgasm. You gotta make things right for her.'

The guy says, 'Well, as much as I would love free beer, I won't do it. You have to be nuts to drink a gallon of pepper tequila and then get crazier from there. Well, as time goes on and the man drinks a few, he asks, 'Wherez zat teeqeelah?'

He grabs the gallon of tequilla with both hands, and downs it with a big slurp and tears streaming down his face. Next, he staggers out back and soon all the people inside hear the most frightening roaring and thumping, then silence.

The man staggers back into the bar, his shirt ripped and big scratches all over his body. 'Now,' he says, 'where's that woman with the sore tooth?'

* * * * *

Three men walk into a bar.

After they drink a couple of beers they are ready to leave, but the bartender won't let them unless they have 12 inches of dick between them.

The first guy whips his out and shows 6 inches.

The second guy drops his pants and shows 5 inches.

Finally, the third guy shows his 1 inch dick.

The bartender says 'Ok, that's 12 inches you can go'.

As the're walking away the first guy says to the third, 'Thank god you had a boner or we'd still be there.'

One day a guy walks into a bar. The bartender says 'if you can make that horse over there laugh you can have free drinks for the rest of the night'.

So he says 'ok' and walks over to the horse and whispers something in his ear and he starts laughing and the bartender gives him free drinks for the rest of the night.

The next night the same guy comes back in and the bartender says 'if you can make that horse over there cry I will give you free drinks for the rest of the night.

So he walks over there and does something and the horse starts crying, and the bartender gives him free drinks. Then the bartender asks what the man did to make the horse laugh and what he did to make him cry.

The man says 'To make him laugh I told him I had a bigger dick than he does and to make him cry I showed him'.

* * * * *

A bear goes into a pub and says, 'Can I have a pint of ....Guinness, please?'

The barman says, 'Sure, but why the big pause?'

A rather attractive woman goes up to the bar in a quiet rural pub. She gestures alluringly to the barman who comes over immediately. When he arrives, she seductively signals that he should bring his face close to hers. When he does so, she begins to gently caress his beard which is full and bushy.

'Are you the Manager?' she asks, softly stroking his face with both hands.

'Actually, no,' he replies.

'Can you get him for me? I need to speak to him,' she asks, running her hands up beyond his beard and into his hair.

'I'm afraid I can't,' breathes the barman—clearly aroused. 'Is there anything I can do?'

'Yes there is. I need you to give him a message,' she continues huskily, popping a couple of fingers into his mouth and allowing him to suck them gently.

'Tell him that there is no toilet paper in the ladies room.'

Hello Sailor

By the time the sailor pulled into a little town, every hotel room was taken.

'You've got to have a room somewhere,' he pleaded. 'Or just a bed, I don't care where.'

'Well, I do have a double room with one occupant—an Air Force guy,' admitted the manager, '... and he might be glad to split the cost. But to tell you the truth, he snores so loudly that people in adjoining rooms have complained in the past. I'm not sure it'd be worth it to you.'

'No problem,' the tired Navy man assured him. 'I'll take it.'

The next morning the sailor came down to breakfast bright-eyed and bushy-tailed.

'How'd you sleep?' asked the manager.

'Never better.'

The manager was impressed. 'No problem with the other guy snoring?'

'Nope, I quieted him in no time' said the Navy guy.

'How'd you manage that?' asked the manager.

'He was already in bed, snoring away, when I came in the

room,' the sailor explained. 'I went over, gave him a kiss on the cheek, and said, 'Goodnight, Beautiful,' and he sat up all night watching me.'

* * * * *

A lady at the far end of the bar waves her arm to get the attention of the waiter and in doing so shows a good hairy underarm.

Down the other end of the bar is a very drunken man.

'Hey waiter get that ballerina a drink on me.'

'How do you know she's a ballerina?'

'Well no one else can get their leg that high.'

* * * * *

A man is waiting while his wife gives birth. The doctor comes out of the theatre afterwards and informs the father that his son was born without arms, legs, or even a torso —his son is just a head! But the dad loves his son and raises him as well as he can, with love and compassion. After 18 years, the son is old enough for his first drink.

Dad takes him to the pub and tearfully tells his son he is proud of him. Dad orders up the biggest strongest drink for his son. With all the patrons looking on curiously and the barman shaking his head in disbelief, the boy takes his first sip of alcohol. Swoosh—a torso pops out!

The bar is dead silent, then bursts into a whoop of joy. The father, shocked, begs his son to drink again. The patrons chant 'Drink! Drink! Drink!' The barman still shakes his head in dismay. Swoosh—two arms pop out!

The bar goes wild. The father, crying and wailing, begs his son to drink again. The patrons chant 'Drink! Drink! Drink!' The barman ignores the whole affair. By now the son is getting tipsy, and with his new hands he reaches down, grabs his drink, and guzzles the last of it. Swoosh—Two legs pop out!

The bar is in chaos. The father thanks God. The boy stands up on his new legs and stumbles to the left... then to the right... then through the front door, into the street, where a truck runs into him and kills him.

The bar falls silent. The father moans in grief. And the barman cleans his glasses and whistles an old Irish tune.

The father looks at the barman in disbelief and asks, 'How can you be so cold and callous?'

'That boy should have quit while he was a head,' the barman replies.

There are three guys drinking in a pub, when another man comes in and starts drinking at the bar. After a while, he approaches the group of lads and pointing at the one in the middle shouts, 'I've shagged your mum!'

The three guys look bewildered as the man resumes his drinking at the bar. Ten minutes later he comes back. 'Your mum's sucked my cock!'

The same thing happens—he then continues to drink, alone at the bar.

Ten minutes later he's back again and announces, 'Oi! I've had your mum up the arse!'

By now the young guys have had enough and the one in the middle can't take it any more. He stands up and shouts, 'Look dad, you're drunk, now piss off home!'

* * * * *

Doggone it

There were two buddies, one with a Doberman Pinscher and the other with a Chihuahua. The guy with the Doberman Pinscher says to his friend, 'Let's go over to that restaurant and get something to eat.'

The guy with the Chihuahua says,' We can't go in there. We've got dogs with us.'

The buddy with the Doberman Pinscher says, 'Just follow my lead.'

They walk over to the restaurant, the guy with the Doberman Pinscher puts on a pair of dark glasses, and he starts to walk in. The bouncer at the door says, 'Sorry, Mac, no pets allowed.'

The man with the Doberman Pinscher says, 'You don't understand. This is my seeing-eye-dog.'

The bouncer says, 'A Doberman Pinscher?'

He says, 'Yes, they're using them now, they're very good and protect me from robbers, too.'

The man at the door says, 'Come on in.'

The buddy with the Chihuahua figures, 'What the heck,' so he puts on a pair of dark glasses and starts to walk in.

Once again the bouncer says, 'Sorry, pal, no pets allowed.'

The guy with the Chihuahua says, 'You don't understand. This is my seeing-eye dog.'

The bouncer at the door says, ' A Chihuahua?'

The man with the Chihuahua says, 'A Chihuahua? They gave me a Chihuahua?'

* * * * *

It Ain't Paddy

Paddy died in a fire and was burnt pretty badly and the morgue needed someone to identify the body. So his two best friends, Dermot and Tony, were sent for.

Dermot went in and the mortician pulled back the sheet.

Dermot said 'Yup, he's burnt pretty bad. Roll him over.'

So the mortician rolled him over and Dermot looked and said 'Nope, it ain't Paddy.'

The mortician thought that was rather strange and then he brought Tony to identify the body.

Tony took a look at him and said, 'Yup, he's burnt real bad, roll him over.'

The mortician rolled him over and Tony looked down and said, 'No, it ain't Paddy.'

The mortician asked, 'How can you tell?'

Tony said, 'Well, Paddy had two assholes.'

'What? He had two assholes?' said the mortician.

'Yup, everyone knew he had two assholes. Every time we went into town, folks would say, 'Here comes Paddy with them two assholes.'

Two men are talking in the pub and one says to the other. 'I'll never forget the time I turned to the bottle as a substitute for women.'

'Why's that then,?' says his mate.

'I got my dick stuck in it.'

A man walks into his local and gets and seat at the bar next to a very drunken man. For some ten minutes the drunk keeps looking at something in his hand and keeps on muttering to himself.

Eventually the mans curiosity gets the better of him and he asks what it is.

'Its odd,' says the drunk, 'it looks like plastic but feels like rubber'.

'Let me see,' says the man.

He takes the object and begins to roll it between his fingers.

'You're right,' he says, 'It does feel like rubber but looks like plastic. Where did you get it from?'

'My nose', replies the drunk.

* * * * *

A white horse walks into a pub and orders a pint of bitter.

'Do you know we have a drink named after you?' said the barman.

'What? George!' says the horse.

A scruffy looking man goes into the pub and orders a pint of bitter.

'Wait a minute,' says the landlord. 'Let me see the cash first.'

'I don't have any money, but if you give me a free pint I promise to fart Blue Suede Shoes for you.'

Intrigued the landlord agrees. The man drinks his pint then hops onto the bar and drop's his trousers to a loud cheer from the locals, he then starts to shit all over the counter.

'Aaagh, you dirty bastard' shouts the landlord. 'I thought you were going to fart Blue Suede Shoes.'

'Now wait a minute,' says the man. 'Even Frank Sinatra had to clear his throat before he began to sing.'

* * * * *

A prominent Welsh minister travelling home one night was greatly annoyed when a young man much the worse for drink came and sat next to him on the bus.

'Young man,' he declared, 'do you not realise you are on the road to perdition?'

'Oh, Hell,' replied the drunkard, 'I could have sworn this bus went to Llanelli.'

Signs you have a hangover:

* You're convinced that chirping birds are Satan's pets.
* Trying to gain control of the situation, you continue to tell your room to 'stay still'.
*Looking at yourself in the mirror induces the same reaction as chugging a glass of fresh paint.
*You'd rather have a pencil jammed up your nose than be exposed to sunlight.
* You set aside an entire morning to spend some quality time with your toilet.
* You replace the traditional praying on your knees with the more feasible praying in a fetal position.
* The bathroom reminds you of a carnival barker shouting, 'Step right up and give it whirl!'
* All day long your motto is, 'Never again.'
* You could purchase a new bike just by recycling the bottles around your bed.
* Your natural response to 'Good morning,' is 'Shut up!'

There was a man who would come home blind drunk every night and vomit in the bathroom sink, and every night the man's wife would warn him that someday he would puke up his guts.

One day his wife cut up a chicken and left the guts in the sink, just to give him a scare. At about 3:00 a.m. the man came home and spewed in the same sink as always. About 30 minutes later, the man came out of the bathroom and said to his wife, 'You were right honey, I really did puke up my guts, but don't worry, with the help of this long wooden spoon, I managed to put them all back.'

* * * * *

A sidewalk and a road have a drink in a pub when a thin piece of taramac goes up to the bar. The sidewalk leans across to the road and whispers 'Stay out of his way, he's a cyclepath.'

A colleague approached this man at lunch and invited him out for a few beers after work. The man said that his wife would never go for it, and that she does not allow him to go drinking with the guys after work.

The colleague suggested a way to overcome that problem: 'When you get home tonight, sneak into the house, slide down under the sheets, gently pull down your wife's panties, and give her oral sex. Women love it, and believe me, she'll never mention that you were out late with the boys.'

So the man agreed to try it, and went out and enjoyed himself.

Late that night, he sneaked into the house, slid down under the sheets, gently slid down his wife's panties, and gave her oral sex. She moaned and groaned with pleasure, but after a little while, he realised he had to take a leak, so he told her he'd be right back, got out of bed and walked down the hall to the bathroom.

When he opened the door and went in, he was very surprised to see his wife sitting on the john.

'How did you get in here?' he asked.

'Shhh!' she replied, 'you'll wake-up my mother!'

A guy walks into a bar carrying an 18 inch alligator.

The bartender says, 'What do think you're doing? Get that goddamn thing out of here. I don't allow pets in my establishment'.

The guy tries to explain. 'Look he won't cause any trouble. He's well trained and I'll prove it'. He then proceeds to put the alligator on the bar and says, 'open'.

The alligator open its mouth and you can see all of its razor sharp teeth. 'Now watch this', he says and proceeds to remove his penis through his zipper and lays his balls gently onto the alligator's teeth.

He then orders a beer and proceeds to drink it. All the while the alligator keeps its mouth open and nothing happens. After finishing the beer the man gently removes his penis and puts it back into his pants.

He then says, 'close' and the alligator closes its mouth. 'You see he is perfectly trained. He would do that for anybody. Does anyone want to try?'

After looking around he finally hears a drunk whose sitting at table say, 'Sure I'd like to try. But I don't know if I can keep my mouth open that long.'

There was this little guy sitting inside a bar, just looking at his drink. After he didn't move for a half-an-hour, this big trouble-making truck driver stepped up right next to him, took the drink from the guy, and just drank it all down. The poor man started crying.

The truck driver turned and said: 'Come on man, I was just joking. Here, I'll buy you another drink. I just can't stand to see a man crying.'

'No, it's not that.' the man replied, 'Today is the worst day of my life. First, I overslept and was late for an important meeting. My boss became outraged and then fired me.

When I left the building to my car, I found out that it was stolen. The police said they could do nothing. I then got a cab to return home, and after I paid the cab driver and the cab had gone, I found that I left my whole wallet in the cab.

I got home only to find my wife was in bed with the gardener.'

The man was really sobbing now, 'I left home depressed and came to this bar. And now, just when I was thinking about putting an end to my life, YOU show up and drink my poison!'

The Beer Prayer

Our lager,
Which art in barrels,
Hallowed be thy drink.
Thy will be drunk,
(I will be drunk),
At home as in the tavern.
Give us this day our foamy head,
And forgive us our spillages,
As we forgive those who spill against us.
And lead us not to incarceration,
But deliver us from hangovers.
For thine is the beer,
The bitter and the lager.
Forever and ever,
Barmen

A lady walks into a bar and says, "Barkeep, gimme a martooni." The bartender goes back and fixes her a martini. She downs it and says, "Barkeep, gimme another martooni." So he goes back and fixes her another martini. She downs that, and just sits there and doesn't say anything. Finally after about 10 minutes bartender says, "Would you like another?"

She says, "Oh, no, I got this terrible heartburn."

The bartender says, "Okay, there are three things wrong here:

Number 1: It's martini, not martooni.

Number 2: It's bartender, not barkeep, and

Number 3: You're not having heartburn, your boob's in the ash tray."

* * * * *

The bartender asks the guy sitting at the bar, 'What'll you have?'

The guy answers, 'A scotch, please.' The bartender hands him the drink, and says 'That'll be five dollars.' The guy replies, 'What are you talking about? I don't owe you anything for this.'

A lawyer, sitting nearby and overhearing the conversation, then says to the bartender, 'You know, he's got you there. In the original offer, which constitutes a binding contract upon acceptance, there was no stipulation of remuneration.'

The bartender says, 'Okay, you beat me for a drink. But don't ever let me catch you in here again.'

The next day, same guy walks into the bar. Bartender says, 'What the heck are you doing in here? I can't believe you've got the audacity to come back!'

The guy says, 'What are you talking about? I've never been in this place in my life!'

The bartender replies, 'I'm very sorry, but this is uncanny. You must have a double.'

To which the guy replies, 'Thank you. Make it a scotch.'

A drunk staggers into a bar, bumping into customers and spilling drinks as he makes his way to the bar. The bartender sees what is going on and is pissed at the drunk when he finally makes it to the bar. 'Get out of here!' says the bartender.

'I gotta go to the baffroom,' slurs the drunk.

'I said get the hell outta here or I'll throw you out!!' yells the bartender.

'I gotta go baffroom,' says the drunk and starts to drop his drawers.

'Hold on, hold on,' says the bartender. 'Alright, you can go to the bathroom, but afterwards you get the hell out of my bar!'

The drunk agrees and stumbles off to the bathroom. After about 5 minutes, everyone hears this loud scream. Dead silence in the bar. Another loud scream from the bathroom. The bartender and a few customers run to the bathroom. There's the drunk sitting down.

'What the hell is going on?' asks the bartender.

'I went, and every time I try to flush the toilet, it crushes my nuts!' says the drunk.

'Why, you stupid shit!' said the bartender. 'You're sitting on my mop bucket!'

* * * * *

A guy walks into a bar and tells everyone there, 'Give me all your money, watches, jewelry and anything else of value or I will inject you with the AIDS virus.' Then he produces a syringe. One by one everyone hands over all their stuff except one man at the end of the bar.

'I told you to hand over all your stuff or I'll inject you with the AIDS virus.'

The man at the bar says, 'Go ahead, I'm wearing a condom.'

* * * * *

Two hydrogen atoms walk into a pub. One says to the other, 'I think I've lost an electron!'

The other says, 'Are you sure?' and the other replies, 'Yes, I'm positive.'

Three guys sitting in a bar around a log fire with their dogs and get talking' about them.

First one says, 'My dog is called Woodworker—go Woodworker.'

The dog grabs a log from the fire with his teeth and paws fashions a beautiful figurine.

Next one says, 'My dog is called Stoneworker—go Stoneworker'

The dog drags a rock from the fire front and a beautiful carving emerges.

Third one says, 'My dog is called Iron Worker' he puts the fire tongs into the fire and gets them red hot. 'Now,' he says, 'I'll just touch him on the balls and you watch him make a bolt for the door.'

* * * * *

A cowboy walks into a bar, dressed entirely in paper. Wasn't long before he was arrested for rustling.

A guy goes into the bar and sits down and orders a drink. Other than the bartender, there's no one else in the place.

All of a sudden he hears a voice say, 'Nice suit.' He looks around and doesn't see anyone and the bartender looks busy washing some glasses. A little while later the same voice says, 'Nice tie.' The guy looks around again and doesn't see anyone. He finally asks the bartender if he just said something.

'No,' replied the bartender, 'it wasn't me. It was probably the peanuts though. They're complimentary.'

* * * * *

A guy walks into a bar, and there's a horse behind the bar serving drinks. The guy is staring at the horse, when the horse says, 'Hey buddy? What are you staring at? Haven't you ever seen a horse serving drinks before?'

The guy says, 'No, it's not that... it's just that I never thought the parrot would sell the place.'

A man was sitting at the bar in a watering hole whose selling point was that it was on top of the largest skyscraper in town. Another man walks in and asks the bartender for a Jack Daniel's. He downs it, and then takes a running leap out the window. Much to everybody's surprise, he floats back up and climbs through the window back into the bar. The man at the bar is amazed and asks the man how he did it.

'Easy,' says the man. 'Outside this window are some very strong wind currents which can carry you back to the window.'

'Wow,' says the man at the bar. 'I gotta try this.' He takes a running leap out the window and falls to a horrible, bloody and flat death.

'Geez, Superman,' says the bartender. 'You can be a real a jerk when you're drunk.'

* * * * *

Shakespeare walks into a pub.

The landlord says, 'Get out—you bard!'

Sister Mary Katherine lived in a convent, a block away from Jack's liquor store. One day, in walked Sister Mary Katherine and she said, 'Oh Jack, give me a pint o' the brandy.'

'Sister Mary Katherine,' exclaimed Jack, 'I could never do that! I've never sold alcohol to a nun in my life!'

'Oh Jack,' she responded, 'it's only for the Mother Superior.' Her voice dropped. 'It helps her constipation, you know.'

So, Jack sold her the brandy. Later that night Jack closed the store and walked home. As he passed the convent, who should he see but Sister Mary Katherine; and she was snookered. She was singing and dancing, whirling around and flapping her arms like a bird, right there on the sidewalk. A crowd was gathering, so Jack pushed through and exclaimed, 'Sister Mary Katherine! For shame! You told me this was for the Mother Superior's constipation!'

Sister Mary Katherine didn't miss a beat as she replied: 'And so it is, me lad, so it is. When she sees me, she's going to shit!'

A physically large guy meets a woman at a bar, and after a number of drinks, they agree to go back to his place.

As they are making out in the bedroom, ready for the act, he stands up and starts to undress. After he takes his shirt off, he flexes his muscular arms and says, 'See there, baby? That's 1000 pounds of Dynamite!'

She begins to drool. The man drops his pants, strikes a bodybuilder's pose, and says, referring to his bulging legs, 'See those, baby? That's 1000 pounds of dynamite!' She is aching for action at this point.

Finally, he drops his underpants, and she grabs her purse and runs screaming to the front door.

He catches her before she is able to run out the door, and asks, 'Why are you in such a hurry to leave?'

She replies, 'With 2000 pounds of dynamite, and such a short fuse, I was afraid you were about to blow!'

* * * * *

Two drunks are walking along the road in London. One turns to the other and slurs, 'Is this Wembley?'

'No, it's Thursday.'

'So am I! Let's go for a drink.'

Hospital Visit

An extremely modest man was in the hospital for a series of tests, the last of which had left his system upset. Upon making several false-alarm trips to the bathroom he decided the latest was another and stayed put.

He suddenly filled his bed with diarrhoea and was embarrassed beyond his ability to remain rational.

Losing his presence of mind, he jumped up, gathered up the bed sheets, and threw them out the window.

A drunk was walking by the hospital when the sheets landed on him. He started yelling, cursing, and swinging his arms wildly, which left the soiled sheets in a tangled pile at his feet.

As the drunk stood there staring down at the sheets, a security guard who had watched the whole incident walked up and asked 'What the hell was that all about?'

Still staring down, the drunk replied, 'I think I just beat the shit out of a ghost!'

A mangy looking guy goes into a bar and orders a drink. The bartender says, 'No way, pal. I don't think you can pay for it.'

'You're right,' the guy says. 'I don't have any money, but if I show you something you haven't seen before, will you give me a drink?'

'You have a deal, my friend,' says the bartender.

The guy reaches into his coat pocket and pulls out a hamster. He puts the hamster on the bar and it runs to the end of the bar, down the side of the bar, across the room, up the piano, onto the keyboard and starts playing Gershwin music. The hamster can really play...

'You're right! I've never seen anything like that before,' says the bartender. 'That hamster is really gifted.'

The guy downs the drink and asks the bartender for another. 'Will that be cash or another miracle, pal?' asks the bartender.

'Watch this,' replies the guy. Again, he reaches into his coat again and pulls out a frog. He puts the frog onto the bar, and the frog starts to sing. The frog has a marvellous voice and great pitch. A fine singer. A stranger from the other end of the bar runs over to the guy and offers him $300 for the frog.

'It's a deal,' says the guy. He takes the three hundred and gives the stranger the frog. The stranger runs out of the bar.

'Are you some kind of nut?' asks the bartender. 'You sold a singing frog for $300? It could have been worth millions. You must be crazy.'

'Not so,' says the guy. 'The hamster is a ventriloquist.'

* * * * *

A drunken man staggered into a Catholic church, sat down in the Confessional and said nothing.

The priest is waiting and waiting and waiting.

The priest coughs to attract the drunk man's attention, but still the man says nothing. The priest then knocks on the wall three times in a final attempt to get the man to speak. Finally the drunk replies, 'No use knockin,' pal. There's no paper.'

Saint Patrick's Day bar troubleshooting

SYMPTOM: Drinking fails to give taste and satisfaction, beer is unusually pale and clear.
FAULT: Glass empty.
ACTION: Find someone who will buy you another beer.

SYMPTOM: Drinking fails to give taste and satisfaction, and the front of your shirt is wet.
FAULT: Mouth not open when drinking or glass applied to wrong part of face.
ACTION: Buy another beer and practice in front of mirror. Drink as many as needed to perfect drinking technique.

SYMPTOM: Feet cold and wet.
FAULT: Glass being held at incorrect angle.
ACTION: Turn glass other way up so that open end points toward ceiling.

SYMPTOM: Feet warm and wet.
FAULT: Improper bladder control.
ACTION: Go stand next to nearest dog. After a while complain to the owner about its lack of house training and demand a beer as compensation.

SYMPTOM: Floor blurred.
FAULT: You are looking through bottom of empty glass.
ACTION: Find someone who will buy you another beer.

SYMPTOM: Floor swaying.
FAULT: Excessive air turbulence, perhaps due to air-hockey game in progress.
ACTION: Insert broom handle down back of jacket.

SYMPTOM: Floor moving.
FAULT: You are being carried out.
ACTION: Find out if you are being taken to another bar. If not, complain loudly that you are being kidnapped.

SYMPTOM: Opposite wall covered with ceiling tiles and fluorescent light strip across it.
FAULT: You have fallen over backward.
ACTION: If your glass is full and no one is standing on your drinking arm, stay put. If not, get someone to help you get up, latch yourself to bar.

SYMPTOM: Everything has gone dim, mouth full of cigarette butts.
FAULT: You have fallen forward.
ACTION: See above.

SYMPTOM: Everything has gone dark.
FAULT: The Bar is closing.
ACTION: Panic.

SYMPTOM: You awaken to find your bed hard, cold and wet. You cannot see your bedroom.
FAULT: You have spent the night in the gutter.
ACTION: Check your watch to see if bars are open yet. If not, treat yourself to a lie-in.

* * * * *

An old guy walks into a bar and asks for a bottle of forty-year old Scotch. The bartender, not wanting to give up the good liquor, pours a shot of ten-year Scotch and figures that the guy won't be able to tell the difference. The guy downs the Scotch and says: 'This Scotch is only ten years old! I specifically asked for forty-year old Scotch.'

Amazed, the bartender reaches into a locked cabinet underneath the bar and pulls out a bottle of twenty-year old Scotch and pours the man a shot. The guy drinks it down and says, 'That was twenty-year old Scotch. I asked for forty-year old Scotch.'

So the bartender goes into the back room and brings out a bottle of thirty-year old Scotch and pours the guy a drink.

By now a small crowd has gathered around the man and is watching anxiously as he downs the latest drink. Once again the guy states the true age of the Scotch and repeats his original request for forty-year old Scotch.

The bartender can hold off no longer and disappears into the cellar to get a bottle of prime forty-year old Scotch. Soon, the bartender returns with the bottle and pours a shot. The guy downs the Scotch and says, 'Now this is forty-year old Scotch!' The crowd applauds his discriminating palate.

An old drunk who had been watching the proceedings with interest, raises a full shot glass of his own and says, 'Here, take a swig of this.'

The guy takes the glass and downs the drink in one swallow. Immediately, he chokes and spits out the liquid on the bar room floor. 'My God! That tastes like piss,' he yells.

'Great guess,' says the drunk. 'Now, how old am I?'

A man walks into a pub with a brace around his neck. He asks for a pint. The bartender gives him one.

Then the man asks, 'Who's in the lounge?'

The bartender replies, '15 people playing darts.'

The man says, 'Get them a pint too.'

Then he asks, 'Who's upstairs?'

The bartender replies, '150 people at the disco.'

The man says, 'Get them a drink too.'

The bartender says, 'That will be $328 please.'

The man says, 'Sorry but I haven't got that much money on me.'

The bartender says, 'If you were at the pub a mile from here, they would have broken your neck.'

The man says, 'I've all ready been there.'

A guy walked into a bar carrying a 12 inch midget. He was a little drunk, so when he told people that the midget was a pianist, nobody believed him. He set the midget down at the piano and the midget started to play. Another guy walked up and stated, 'Hey, he's pretty good, where did you find him?'

'In the dumpster in the alley out back is a red bottle, rub the bottle and a genie will come out. He'll give you one wish.' The man replied. So the other guy went out into the alley, jumped into the dumpster, and found the bottle. Sure enough, a genie came out. 'I will give you one wish, for whatever you want.' The genie announced.

The man thought, and finally, he made up his mind. 'I want a million bucks!' he declared with a slur in his voice. (he too was a little drunk) Suddenly, a huge flock of ducks flew over, scattering their droppings all over him. This really ticked the guy off. He ran into the bar, grabbed the guy with the pianist buy the collar, and demanded to know why the genie had given him a million ducks instead of a million bucks.

'Hey, you don't think I asked for a 12 inch pianist, do you?'

A guy walks into a bar and he orders a whiskey. He sits down and just before he takes a sip of his whiskey a guy runs in and says, 'Bill! Your house burnt down!'

So he runs outside but then he thinks, 'I don't have a house.' So he goes back into the bar and takes a sip of his whiskey.

Another guy runs in and says, 'Bill! Your dad died!'

And so he runs out of the bar, gets on his horse and rides a little ways but then thinks, 'I don't have a dad.'

So he goes back into the bar and drinks almost all of his whiskey when another guy runs in and says, 'Bill! You won the lottery!'

So he runs out, gets on his horse and rides all the way to the bank but then thinks, 'My name's not Bill.'

* * * * *

...A snake slithers into a bar and the bartender says, 'I'm sorry but I can't serve you.'

'Why not?' asks the snake.

The bartender says, 'Because you can't hold your liquor...'

An Irish man shows up in a pub one day and orders three pints of Guinness. He takes sips from each glass until they are empty and calls the bartender for three more. The bartender says, 'Sure it's up to yourself, but wouldn't you rather I was bringing them one at a time? Then they'll be fresh and cold.'

'Nah...' your man says, 'I'm preferrin' that ye bring 'em three at a time. You see, me and me two brothers would meet at a pub and drink and have good times. Now one is in Australia, the other in Canada and I'm here. We agreed before we split up that we'd drink to each other's honour this way.'

'Well,' says the bartender, 'that's a grand thing to do, all right. I'll bring the pints as you ask.'

Well, time goes on and the man's peculiar habit is known and accepted by all the pub's regulars. One day though, he orders only two pints. A hush falls over the pub. Naturally, everyone figures something happened to one of the brothers. A group of the regulars corner the bartender and finally persuade him to find out what happened. With a heavy heart, the bartender brings the two pints and says, 'Here's your pints... and let me offer my sincerest condolences. What happened?'

The Irish man looks extremely puzzled for a moment, and then starts laughing.

'Oh, no, no, no! 'Tis nothing like that. You see, I've given up drinking for Lent...'

* * * * *

A fellow walks into a bar very down on himself. Walking to the bar the bartender asks, 'What's the matter?'

The fellow replies, 'Well I've got these two horses (sniff, sniff), and well... I can't tell them apart. I don't know if I'm mixing up riding times or even feeding them the right foods.'

The bartender, feeling sorry for the guy, tries to think of somthing he can do. 'Why don't you try shaving the tail of one of the horses?'

The man stops crying and says, 'That sounds like a good idea, I think I'll try it.'

A few months later he comes back to the bar in worse condition than he was before. 'What's the matter now?' the bartender asks.

The fellow, in no condition to be in public, answers, 'I

shaved the tail of one of the horses (sob, sob), but it grew back and I can't tell them apart again!'

The bartender, now just wanting him to shut up or leave says, 'why don't you try shaving the mane, maybe that will not grow back.'

The fellow stops crying, has a few drinks, and leaves. A few months later the fellow is back in the bar. The bartender has never seen anybody in such a sorry state. Without the bartender even asking the fellow breaks into his problems. 'I... I shaved the (sob) mane of one of the (sniff) horses, and... it... it... grew back!'

The bartenter, now furious at the guy's general stupidity, yells, 'For crying out loud, just measure the stupid horses. Perhaps one is slightly taller that the other one!' The fellow can not believe what the bartender has said and storms out of the bar.

The next day the fellow comes running back into the bar as if he had just won the lottery. 'It worked, it worked!' he exclaims. 'I measured the horses and the black one is two inches taller than the white one!'

The bartender was washing his glasses when an elderly Irishman came in. With great difficulty, the Irishman hoisted his bad leg over the barstool, pulled himself up painfully, and asked for a sip of Irish whiskey.

The Irishman looked down the bar and asked, 'Is that Jesus down there?'

The bartender nodded, so the Irishman told him to give Jesus an Irish whiskey, too.

The next patron to come in was an ailing Italian with a hunched back, who moved very slowly. He shuffled to the bar stool and asked for a glass of Chianti.

He also looked down the bar and asked, 'Is that Jesus sitting at the end of the bar?'

The bartender nodded, so the Italian said to give Him a glass of Chianti.

The third patron to enter the bar was a redneck, who swaggered into the bar and hollered, 'Barkeep, set me up a cold one!'

'Hey, is that God's Boy down there?'

The barkeep nodded, so the redneck told him to give Jesus a cold one.

As Jesus got up to leave, he walked over to the Irishman and touched him and said, 'For your kindness, you are healed!'

The Irishman felt the strength come back to his leg, so he got up and danced a jig out the door.

Jesus touched the Italian and said, 'For your kindness, you are healed!'

The Italian felt his back straighten, so he raised his hands above his head and did a flip out the door.

Jesus walked toward the redneck, but the redneck jumped back and exclaimed, 'Don't touch me! I'm drawing disability!'

* * * * *

A dog walks into a bar. He hops onto a bar stool and puts his front paws on the bar. He looks the bartender right in the eye and says, 'Hey, guess what? I'm a talking dog. Have you ever seen a talking dog before? How about a drink for the talking dog?'

The bartender thinks for a moment and says, 'Alright. The toilet's right around the corner.'

A man in a bar has a couple of beers, and the bartender tells him he owes $8.

'But I already paid you! Don't you remember?' says the customer.

'Okay,' says the bartender, 'if you said you paid, then I suppose you did.'

The man then goes outside and tells the first person he sees that the bartender can't keep track of whether his customers have paid or not. The second man then rushes in, orders a beer, and later pulls the same stunt.

The barkeep replies, 'Okay, if you said you paid, then I suppose you did.'

The customer then goes outside, sees a friend, and tells him how to get free drinks.The third man hurries into the bar and begins to drink highballs. Some time later, the bartender leans over and says, 'You know, a funny thing happened in here tonight. Two men were drinking beer, neither paid, and both claimed that they had paid. The next guy who tries that stunt is going to get his butt kicked.'

The man interrupts, 'Don't bother me with your troubles, bartender. Just give me my change and I'll be on my way.'

A man in a bar sees a friend at a table, drinking by himself.

Approaching the friend he comments, "You look terrible. What's the problem?"

"My mother died in August," he said, "and left me $25,000."

"Gee, that's tough," he replied.

"Then in September," the friend continued, "My father died, leaving me $90,000."

"Wow. Two parents gone in two months. No wonder you're depressed."

"And last month my aunt died, and left me $15,000."

"Three close family members lost in three months? How sad."

"Then this month," continued the friend, "absolutely nothing!"

* * * * *

A man walks into a bar, sits down on a bench and orders a cold one. He swigs down the beer, looks in his pocket, cringes and orders another. He gulps down that one, looks in his pocket again, cringes and orders yet another one. This goes on for at least an hour and a half.

Finally the bartender, bursting with curiousity, says, 'I know it's none of my business buddy, but I have to ask. Why the whole "drink, look in pocket, cringe and order another one" routine?'

'Well,' slurred the man, 'There's a picture of my wife in my pocket. When she starts to look good, then it's time for me to go home.'

* * * * *

A man and his pet giraffe walk into a bar and start having a few quiet drinks. As the night goes on, they get pretty drunk. The giraffe finally passes out near the pool tables, and the man decides to go home.

As the man is leaving, he's approached by the barman who says, 'Hey, you're not gonna leave that lyin' here, are ya?'

'Hmph,' says the man, 'that's not a lion, it's a giraffe.'

A drunk staggers into a bar and says to the bartender, 'I'd like to buy everyone in the bar a drink and get one for yourself too!'

The bartender makes the drinks and everyone raises their glass and yells 'CHEERS!' and downs their drinks.

The bartender says, 'That'll be $37.50.'

The drunk says, 'Kiss my big white ass, 'cuz I don't have any money!'

This infuriates the bartender who then jumps over the bar and beats the living hell out of the drunk and throws him out into the street.

The next day the same drunk walks into the same bar and says, 'I'd like to buy the whole bar a drink, and get one for yourself, too'

The bartender figures that maybe he was a little hard on the guy the day before and decides to give the guy the benefit of the doubt. He makes the drinks and they all say, 'Salute!' and down the drinks.

The bartender says, 'That'll be $42,50.'

The drunk replies by putting his thumb to his nose, wiggling his fingers, and making a loud raspberry noise followed by, ‘I don’t have any money and you can kiss my big white ass!’

This angers the bartender even more than the first time. He jumps over the bar and beats the hell out of the drunk and throws him out into the street onto his face and kicks him a few times for good measure.

The next day the same drunk walks into the same bar, but before he can say anything the bartender says, ‘Let me guess, you want to buy the whole bar a drink and I should get one for myself, too, right?’

The drunk replies, ‘No way, you get too violent when you drink!’

* * * * *

A man walks into the pub and order’s a pint of less. ‘A pint of less, is that a new drink asks the barmaid’?

‘I don’t know,’ says the man. ‘I’ve just come from the doctors and he told me I should drink less in future.’

A drunk guy in Alaska decides to go ice fishing. So he packs up his stuff and goes out onto the ice.

He starts sawing a hole in the ice, and a loud booming voice says, 'YOU WILL FIND NO FISH UNDER THAT ICE!'

The drunk looks up, ignores it, and continues on. The voice repeats, 'YOU WILL FIND NO FISH UNDER THE ICE.'

The drunk looks up and says, 'God? Is this God trying to warn me?'

The voice says 'NO, I'M THE MANAGER OF THIS ICE RINK.'

* * * * *

Everyday a man went into his local and he would always be surrounded by gorgeous women.

'I don't understand it,' said the barman to one of the locals, 'he dresses like a tramp he has no money and all he ever does is sit there licking his eyebrows'.

Three mice are sitting at a bar in a pretty rough neighborhood late at night trying to impress each other about how tough they are. The first mouse orders a scotch, gulps it down and slams the glass on the bar. He turns to the second mouse and says, "When I see a mousetrap, I lie on my back and set it off with my foot. When the bar comes down, I catch it in my teeth, bench press it 20 times to work up an appetite, and then make off with the cheese."

The second mouse orders two shots of bourbon, slams them down and nearly breaks the glasses on the bar. He turns to the first mouse and replies, "Yeah, well, when I see rat poison, I collect as much as I can, take it home, grind it into a powder, and add it to my coffee each morning so I can get a good buzz going for the rest of the day."

The first mouse and the second mouse then turn to the third mouse. The third mouse lets out a long sigh and says to the first two, "I don't have time for this BS. I gotta go home and screw the cat."

Dead Doberman

A highly timid little man, ventured into a biker bar in the Bronx and clearing his throat asked, 'Um, err, which of you gentlemen owns the Doberman tied outside to the parking meter?'

A giant of a man, wearing biker leathers, his body hair growing out through the seams, turned slowly on his stool, looked down at the quivering little man and said, 'It's my dog. Why?'

'Well,' squeaked the little man, obviously very nervous, 'I believe my dog just killed it, sir.'

'What?' roared the big man in disbelief. 'What in the hell kind of dog do you have?'

'Sir,' answered the little man, 'It's a four week old puppy.'

'Bull!' roared the biker, 'How could your puppy kill my Doberman?'

'It appears that he choked on it, sir.'

Two men are talking in the pub one night when one say's to the other, 'I was shagging the wife last night and halfway through I muff dived her and blew right up her fanny, she got so excited that she lifted six inches off the bed in ectasy'.

'That's nothing,' said his mate. 'Last night I was shagging the wife and halfway through I picked her up and sat her on my dick and then spun her around like she was on a swivel chair, she got that excited that she lifted ten inches off the bed in ectasy'.

'That's nothing lads,' said a old guy of about seventy who had been listening to their conversation, 'Last night I was shagging the wife and when I'd finished I wiped my dick on her new nightie, and she nearly hit the fucking roof'.

* * * * *

There was this duck that walked into a bar and sat down on a stool and the bartender said, 'Can I help you?'

The duck said, 'Quack, quack, quack, got any raisins?'

The bartender said, 'No! This is a bar and we don't sell raisins.'

The duck walked out and then he came in the next day and sat on the very same stool!

The bartender walked over and asked him if he could help him? The duck said, 'Quack, quack, quack, got any raisins?'

The bartender said, 'No, this is a BAR we don't sell raisins!' So the duck walked out again and left.

He came back the next day and sat on the same stool once again! The duck yelled at the bartender, 'Quack, quack, quack, got any raisins?'

The bartender said, 'No. And if you come back here once more I am gonna nail your webbed feet to the ground and you are gonna die there.' The duck said, 'ok', and left.

The next day came and sure enough the duck came back except he only peeped his head inside the door. He said, 'Quack, quack, got any nails?' The bartender replied, 'No!'

The duck said, 'Good, then you got any raisins?'

A horse walks into a bar, orders a beer, sits down at one of the tables, and starts reading his paper. The bartender is a bit shocked by all this, but pours the beer, and brings it over to the horse, who proffers a ten dollar bill for it.

Now the barman figures the horse isn't that bright, so he decides to pull the old 'short-change' trick on him. He duly goes back to the horse with one dollar. The horse doesn't say a word. The horse eventually finishes his beer and goes up to the bar to order another.

The bartender says to him, 'you know, we don't get many horses in here.'

To which the horse replies, 'At nine dollars a beer, I'm not surprised!'

* * * * *

A horse walks into a pub.

The landlord says, 'Why the long face?'

An Englishman, a Scotsman and and Irishman are all drinking a guiness at the bar, when all at once a fly drops into each mans pint glass.

The Englishman stands up disgusted, and says 'Barkeep, there is a fly in my beer...I demand a new on!'

The Scotsman...shrugs his shoulders and downs the pint, fly and all...

The Irishman reaches into the pint...pulls out the fly...grabs it by the wings, and starts shaking it violently, screaming...

'SPIT IT OUT DAMN YOU....SPIT IT OUT!'

* * * * *

A policeman stops a motorist and says, 'Excuse me sir, have you been drinking?'
The motorist says, 'Why, have I got a fat girl next to me?'

A guy walks in to a bar with his pet monkey. He orders a drink and while he's drinking the monkey jumps all around the place. The monkey grabs some olives off the bar and eats them. Then he grabs some sliced limes and eats them. Then he jumps on to the pool table, grabs one of the billiard balls, sticks it in his mouth, and to everyone's amazement, and somehow swallows it whole.

The bartender screams at the guy, 'Did you see what your monkey did?'

The guy says, 'No, what?'

'He just ate the cue ball off my pool table—whole!'

'Yeah, that doesn't surprise me,' replied the guy. 'He eats everything in sight, the little bastard. Sorry. I'll pay for everything.'

The man finishes his drink, pays his bill, pays for the stuff the monkey ate and leaves.

Two weeks later, he's in the bar again, and his pet monkey is with him. He orders a drink and the monkey starts running around the bar again.

While the man is finishing his drink, the monkey finds a maraschino cherry on the bar. He grabs it, sticks it up his ass, pulls it out and eats it.

The bartender is disgusted. 'Did you see what your monkey did now?' he asks.

'No, what?' replied the guy.

'Well, he stuck a maraschino cherry up his ass, pulled it out and ate it!' said the bartender.

'Yeah, that doesn't surprise me,' replied the guy. He still eats everything in sight but, ever since he swallowed that cue ball, he measures everything first.'

* * * * *

A drunk is driving through the city and his car is weaving violently all over the road. A cop pulls him over and asks, 'Where have you been?'

'I've been to the pub,' slurs the drunk.

'Well,' says the cop, 'it looks like you've had quite a few.'

'I did alright,' the drunk says with a smile.

'Did you know,' says the cop, standing straight and folding his arms, 'that a few intersections back, your wife fell out of your car?'

'Oh, thank heavens,' sighs the drunk. 'For a minute there, I thought I'd gone deaf.'

A woman in the bar says that she wants to have plastic surgery to enlarge her breasts. Her husband tells her, 'Hey, you don't need surgery to do that. I know how to do it without surgery.'

The lady asks, 'How do I do it without surgery?'

'Just rub toilet paper between them.'

'How does that make them bigger?'

'I don't know, but it worked for your ass.'

* * * * *

A guy has to take a crap really badly so he goes into a bar thinking the bathroom is upstairs. He goes upstairs but can't find the bathroom anywhere. Finding a hole in the floor he takes a crap in it. After that he goes downstairs and finds no one there. He asks the bartender were everyone is?
Responding, the battender says, 'Where the hell were you when shit hit the fan?'

This Scottish farmer walks into the neighbourhood pub, and orders a whiskey.

'Ye see that fence over there?' he says to the bartender. 'Ah built it with me own two hands! Dug up the holes with me shovel, chopped doon the trees for the posts by me ownself, laid every last rail! But do they call me 'McGregor the Fence-Builder?'

No...'

He gulps down the whiskey and orders another. 'Ye see that pier on the loch?' He continues, 'Ah built it me ownself, too. Swam oot into the loch to lay the foondations, laid doon every single board! But do they call me "McGregor the Pier-Builder?"

No.

'But ye fuck ONE sheep....'

* * * * *

A guy walks out of a bar on the moon, complaining 'The drinks were okay but there is no atmosphere.'

This cowboy walks into the saloon and orders a whiskey. The bartender slides it along the bar and the cowboy downs it in one gulp. Immediately he rushes back out the bar, goes to his horse, lifts its tail, and gives it a huge smacking kiss there.

He then goes back into the bar and orders another whiskey. The bartender slides it along the bar and once again the cowboy downs it in one gulp then rushes out the bar, goes to his horse, lifts its tail, and gives it a huge smacking kiss there.

He goes back into the bar and orders another whiskey. By this time there are a number of other patrons looking at him with a fair bit of interest. The bartender decides he'd better ask what's going on before the cowboy gets too drunk to answer.

'So, cowboy, why is it that every time you order a whiskey you go out and kiss your horse on the bum?'

The cowboy (in his best drawl) replies 'Chapped lips.'

The bartender says with some surprise 'Oh, does that cure them?'

The cowboy says 'Nope, but it sure stops me lickin' 'em'.

Two vampires walk into a pub and call for the landlord. 'What'll it be, sir?' asks the landlord.

'I'll have a pint of blood,' says the first vampire. 'Coming up,' says the landlord. 'And for you, sir?' he asks, turning to the other vampire.

'I'll have a pint of plasma,' replies the second vampire. 'Ok,' says the landlord, 'that's one blood and one blood-lite...'

* * * * *

Walking into the bar, Harvey said to the bartender, 'Pour me a stiff one, Eddie. I just had a fight with the little woman.'

'Oh yeah,' said Eddie. 'And how did this one end?'

'When it was over,' Harvey replied, 'she came to me on her hands and knees.'

'Really? Now that's a switch! What did she say?'

'She said, 'Come out from under that bed, you gutless weasel!'

Mick Flaherty had supped more Guinness than enough and had stumbled out of Quinn's bar and into the Sunday afternoon air.

As his drunken eyes squinted to adjust to the light, an ambulance went by at great speed. Blue lights flashing and siren blaring, it roared up the street with Mick in full flight running after it.

A hundred yards, two hundred, three hundred, almost a quarter of a mile he tracked it until suddenly, lungs and legs giving out, he fell into the gutter.

Then with his very last ounce of breath he roared: 'You can keep your damned ice cream!'

* * * * *

Two old friends/enemies who love to take the piss out of each other are in a bar, drinking. One reaches over and feels the other's bald head.

"Good God! This feels just like my wife's ass!" The man whose head it is runs his hand over it, too.

"So it does! So it does!"

Paddy had been drinking at his local Dublin pub all day and most of the night celebrating Ireland's football victory.

Mick, the bartender, says, 'You'll not be drinking any more tonight, Paddy'

Paddy replies, 'OK Mick, I'll be on my way then.' Paddy spins around on his stool and steps off. He falls flat on his face.

'Shoite,' he says and pulls himself up by the stool and dusts himself off.

He takes a step towards the door and falls flat on his face. 'Shoite, Shoite!'

He looks to the doorway and thinks to himself that if he can just get to the door and some fresh air he'll be fine.

He crawls to the door and shimmies up to the door frame, sticks his head outside and takes a deep breath of fresh air,feels much better and takes a step out onto the sidewalk. He falls flat on his face. 'Bi Jesus... I'm fockin' focked,' he says.

He can see his house just a few doors down, and crawls to the door and shimmies up the door frame, opens the door and shimmies inside.

He takes a look up the stairs and says, 'No fockin' way'. He crawls up the stairs to his bedroom door and says, 'If I can just make it to me bed.' He takes a step into the room and falls flat on his face. He says, 'Fock it,' and falls into bed.

The next morning, his wife, Jess, comes into the room carrying a cup of coffee and says, 'Get up Paddy. Did you have a bit to drink last night?'Paddy says, 'I did Jess. I was fockin' p*ssed. But how'd you know?'

Mick called. 'You left your wheelchair at the pub.'

* * * * *

A man walked into a bar and sat down next to a man with a dog at his feet. 'Does your dog bite?' he asked.

'No.' was the reply.

A few minutes later the dog took a huge chunk out of his leg. 'I thought you said your dog doesn't bite!' the man said indignantly.

'That's not my dog.' was the answer.

A drunken guy walks into a bar and puts his money down and orders a bourbon. Several minutes go by and suddenly the drunken guy leans over and tells the bartender, 'Hey, theres a gorilla at the other end of the bar.'

The bartender replies, 'That's my pet gorilla, Mable.'

'I never knew anybody who had a gorilla for a pet,' replied the guy. The bartender then tells the customer 'Watch this,' and calls out, 'Mable, get over here.' Mable comes over to the bartender and while standing in front of the bartender, the bartender reaches behind the bar and grabs a hammer, hits Mable in the head with it. Mable drops to her knees, pulls down the bartenders zipper, takes out his penis and starts sucking it.

The drunken guy is in total shock and exclaims, 'I never saw anything like that before.'

The bartender then asks the drunk 'You want one?' The drunk tells the bartender, 'Ok, but don't hit me on the head so hard!'

A guy walks into a bar with a dog under his arm, puts the dog on the bar and announces that the dog can talk and that he has $100 he's willing to bet anyone who says he can't. The bartender takes the bet and the owner looks at the dog and asks, 'What's the thing on top of this building which keeps the rain from coming inside'. The dog answers, 'ROOF'.

The bartender says 'Who are you kidding, I'm not paying'.

The dogs owner says, 'How about double or nothing and I'll ask him something else'. The bartender agrees and the owner turns to the dog and asks, 'Who was the greatest ballplayer of all time'.

The dog answers, 'Roof'. With that the bartender picks them both up and throws them out the door. As they bounce on the sidewalk the dog looks at his owner and says 'DiMaggio?'

Two rednecks are driving down the highway, drinking their beer, when flashing lights from a policeman appear in the driver's rear-view mirror. "Don't worry!" says the driver to his friend, "Just do exactly what I tell you and everything will work out perfectly. First, we'll peel the labels off our beer bottles and we'll each stick one on our forehead. Now shove all of the bottles under the front seat! And, let me do all the talking!"

They pull over to the side of the road and the cop walks up to the car. He shines his flashlight into the car and looks at the two drunks. "Have you been drinking?" he asks them.

"Oh, no Sir," replies the driver.

"I noticed you weaving back and forth across the highway. Are you sure you haven't been drinking?" the cop asks.

"Oh, no sir," the drunk answers. "We haven't had a thing to drink tonight."

"Well, I've got to ask you," says the cop, "What on earth are those things on your forehead?"

"That's easy, Officer," says the drunk. "You see, we're both alchoholics, and we're on the patch!"

Murphy had been greeted by the stunning news that he was to become a father for the first time. Jumping with joy, he couldn't wait to go out and celebrate with his pals. But first he must tend to the needs of his lovely wife, Kate.

'Now my darling, I'm just popping along the road for a few minutes. Is there anything you'd like while I'm out?'

'Yes Pat,' said Kate. 'I'd like you to buy some snails. I just fancy cooking them in garlic butter tonight. So don't be long will you?'

'I'll be back before you know it,' promised Pat, full of good intentions.

Two hours later, bag of snails in hand, he was still propping up Mooney's bar and wetting the baby's head for the umpteenth time. Finally he decided to do the right thing and bade farewell to his pals and stumbled out into the night. Weaving from side to side, he eventually reached his house and tottered up towards the door. Sadly, in trying to get his keys out of his pocket, he dropped the bag of snails and 'crack' it split open on the step scattering snails everywhere.

The noise woke Kate who opened the bedroom window and shouted down: 'What's going on? Where have you been all this time?'

Murphy looked down at the snails, clapped his hands and said: 'Come on lads—we're nearly home!'

* * * * *

A guy walks into a bar, approaches the bartender and says; 'I've been working on a top-secret project on molecular genetics for the past five years and I've just got to talk to someone about it.'

The bartender says; 'Wait a minute. Before we talk about that, just answer me a few questions: When a deer defecates, why does it come out like little pellets?'

The guy didn't know that. The bartender then asks, 'Why is it that when a dog poops, it lands on the ground and looks like a coiled rope?'

The guy again says, 'I don't have any idea.'

The bartender then says, 'You don't know shit, and you want to talk about molecular genetics?'

A bear walks into a bar and orders a beer... The bartender tells him, 'I don't serve beers to bears in my bar.' The bear, a bit annoyed, insists on his beer. The bartender says, 'Sorry, I don't serve beers to bears in my bar.' So the bear ups to him and says, 'See that woman down there? If you don't give me my beer, I'm going to eat her.' Once again, the bartender says, 'I DON'T SERVE BEER TO BEARS IN MY BAR!'

So the bear ups and goes down to the end of the bar and eats the woman, after which, he sits back on his stool and says, 'See, I told you to give me the beer.' Then the bartender says, 'Listen, I DON'T SERVE BEER TO BEARS IN MY BAR... especially when they've been doing drugs.'

'What?' shouts the bear.

'Yeah, that was a bar bitch you ate.'

* * * * *

A scuffle started in the local one Friday night. Words were exchanged, then insults and finally blows. Bottles, glasses, people, flew through the air and Casey ended up being hit in the face by a sharp piece of glass which cut off his nose.

'Stick his nose back on and hold it with your hand,' ordered McGinty. 'And we'll get him to the hospital.'

Out into the street they flew to be greeted by sheets of rain pelting down.

Quickly they bundled the injured man along and into the casualty department.

'Will he live?' inquired the boys.

'Too late,' said the doctor, 'he's a goner.'

'Was it loss of blood?' asked Finbar.

'No, he drowned. You put his nose on upside down,' sighed the doc.

* * * * *

A termite walked into a bar and said,

"Is the bar tender here?"

A man walked into a Melbourne bar and ordered a pint of the dark liquid.

'Excuse me,' said the only other drinker. 'Is that an Irish accent I detect?'

'It is, sir. Dublin to be exact.'

'Bless my soul,' said the first. 'I'm a Dublin man meself. Ballymun to be precise.'

'Bedad, aren't I from Ballymun meself—Carberry Street in actual fact,' remarked the second.

'Carberry Street is where I was born and raised meself, and St Joseph's was me parish church, Father Dunne the parish priest.'

'Didn't I go to nine o'clock mass every Sunday at St Joseph's. What an amazingly small world. Did you go to St Joseph's School?'

'I did. I was in Miss Slattery's class.'

'God in heaven. So was I.'

Just then the phone rang and the Aussie barman said, 'Not too busy at the moment. In fact there's just the Murphy twins here.'

This guy walks into a small town bar and orders a drink from the bartender.

The bartender delivers his drink and shouts out to the bar patrons, "46!" Everyone starts to laugh—Again he shouts out, "39!"

Now the patrons are getting even louder in laughing—Lastly, he shouts, "14!" Now, people are wiping tears from their eyes from all the laughing.

The visitor is curious, so he asks the bartender, "What is going on?"

The bartender says, "This is a small town, with small impressionable children, and so we had decided to put numbers to our naughty jokes rather than tell them in full."

The visitor is astounded "Let me try!" he says—So he shouts, "46!" Nothing happens, "39!" Still nothing. "14!" and yet still not a sound from the patrons.

The visitor says to the bartender, "I don't understand. I used exactly the same numbers you did and got a completely opposite response.

The bartender replied, "Well, some folks can tell a joke... and some folks can't."

A guy walks into a bar with a ferret on his shoulder, puts it on the bar and asks for a drink. The bartender sees the ferret and says, “Hey buddy, what’s with the ferret?”

The guy says, “I tell ya what pal, this ferret gives the best blowjob on the planet.’

The bartender looks at him and says “Get the fuck outta here and take your rat with you!”

The guy says, “Take the ferret in the back and if your not satisfied, I’m outta here.”

Ten minutes later the bartender comes out of the back room with the ferret, drops it on the bar and says “DAMN, that was the best blowjob I’ve ever had, I’ll give you $500 for it.”

The guy goes “Sorry pal, it’s not for sale.”

The bartender says “I’ll go as high as $2000.”

“SOLD!”, the guy yells, and walks out of the bar.

The bartender quickly closes up, grabs the ferret and heads home. When he opens the door to his house, his wife is standing in the kitchen, she says, “What the hell is that?”

He passes the ferret to his wife and says, “Teach it to cook and get the fuck out!”

An Irishman walks into a bar and asks for two beers. He then pulls a small green-skinned man out of his pocket and puts him on the counter. As he's drinking one drink and the green man is drinking the other, an Englishman down the bar who has had a few too many drinks says, "Hey, what's that little green thing down there?"

The green man runs down the bar gives the Englishman a raspberry, SPLBLBLBLT! right in the face and runs back to the Irishman. The Englishman mops himself off and says to the Irishman, "Hey, what is that thing, anyway?"

The Irishman replies, "Have some respect. He's a leprechaun."

"Oh, all right." the Englishman says sullenly. They all go back to drinking beer.

An hour or so later, the Englishman is really plastered. "Boy, that leprechaun is ugly!" he says. The leprechaun runs down the bar and gives the Englishman a raspberry again, SPLBLBLBLBT! This time the Englishman is really mad! "Tell that leprechaun that if he does that again I'll cut his pecker off!" he shouts.

"You can't do that" says the Irishman. "Leprechauns don't have peckers."

"How do they pee, then?" asks the Englishman.

"They don't." says the Irishman. "They go SPLBLBLBLBLT."

* * * * *

'Wasn't it tragic about my brother Michael,' moaned Kelly. 'Women and whiskey killed him.'

'Is that so?' sympathised O'Toole.

'Yes, he couldn't get either so he hung himself!'

* * * * *

'Have you decided what to buy your missus for Christmas?' asked McPhee.

'Sure, she decided it for me,' answered Kelly. 'She said she wanted something with diamonds in it. So I've bought her a pack of cards!'

* * * * *

'I've bought a new clock,' boasted Clancy. 'It goes eight days without winding.'

'How long does it go if you do wind it?' asked the barman.

A guy walks into a bar with an octopus on his shoulder. The bartender says, "You can't bring that in here!"

The guy says, "Why not? He's a pet. Plus I'll bet you a drink he can play any instrument in here."

The bartender says, "Okay, here's a trombone, I'll bet a drink he can't play it." The octopus picks it up and starts playing a tune. The bartender is a little upset and pulls out a clarinet and says, "I bet another drink he can't play this."

The guy says okay and the octopus picks up the clarinet and starts playing away on it. By now the bartender is really upset. He's had to give the guy two free drinks already. Then he remembers he has an old set of bag-pipes in the back. He tells the guy, "I'll bet you one more drink he can't play something else I have," and throws out the bag-pipes. The octopus takes one look at the set of bagpipes and starts swarming all over it, pulling on the pipes and squeezing the bag.

The bartender laughs and says, "I guess I win."

The guy says, "just give him a minute. As soon as he realises he can't fuck it... he'll play it!"

John was sitting outside his local pub one day, enjoying a quiet pint and generally feeling good about himself, when a nun suddenly appears at his table and starts decrying the evils of drink.

"You should be ashamed of yourself young man! Drinking is a Sin! Alcohol is the blood of the devil!"

Now John gets pretty annoyed about this, and goes on the offensive. "How do you know this, Sister?"

"My Mother Superior told me so."

"But have you ever had a drink yourself? How can you be sure that what you are saying is right?"

"Don't be ridiculous—of course I have never taken alcohol myself"

"Then let me buy you a drink—if you still believe afterwards that it is evil I will give up drink for life"

"How could I, a nun, sit outside this public house drinking?!"

"I'll get the barman to put it in a teacup for you, then no one will ever know."

The nun reluctantly agrees, so John goes inside to the bar.

"Another pint for me, and a triple vodka on the rocks," then he lowers his voice and says to the barman, "and could you put the vodka in a teacup?"

"Oh no! It's not that nun again is it?"

A serious drunk walked into a bar and, after staring for some time at the only woman seated at the bar, walked over to her and kissed her. She jumped up and slapped him silly. He immediately apologized and explained, "I'm sorry. I thought you were my wife. You look exactly like her."

"Why you worthless, insufferable, wretched, no good drunk!" she screamed.

"Funny," he muttered, "you even sound exactly like her."

A man walks into a bar and says, "Bartender, give me two shots."

Bartender says, "You want them both now or one at a time?"

The guy says, "Oh, I want them both now. One's for me and one's for this little guy here," and he pulls a tiny three inch man out of his pocket.

The bartender asks, "He can drink?"

"Oh, sure. He can drink."

So the bartender pours the shots and sure enough, the little guy drinks it all up.

"That's amazing," says the bartender. "What else can he do, can he walk?"

The man flicks a quarter down to the end of the bar and says, "Hey, Jake. Go get that." The little guy runs down to the end of the bar and picks up the quarter. Then he runs back down and gives it to the man.

The bartender is in total shock. "That's amazing," he says, "what else can he do? Does he talk?"

The man says, "Sure he talks, hey, Jake, tell him about that time we were in Africa and you made fun of that witch doctor's powers!"

There was a little guy sitting at a bar drinking a beer. A while later a huge guy walked into the bar and he went up to the little guy and karate chopped him in the back. The little guy fell off his bar stool and when he got up the big guy said, "That was a karate chop from Korea."

The big guy went to the restroom and the little guy ordered himself another beer. About twenty minutes later the big guy came back and karate choped the little guy in the back again. The little guy got up and dusted himself off and the big guy told him, "That was a karate chop from China."

The little guy got up and decided he wasn't going to take any more of this, so he left the bar. About an hour later the little guy comes back to the bar and he hits the big guy in the back. The big guy is knocked out cold and he's on the floor. The little guy tells the bartender, "Tell him that was a crowbar from Sears!"

* * * * *

John Smith lived in Staten Island, New York and worked in Manhattan. He had to take the ferryboat home every night. One evening, he got down to the ferry and found there was a wait for the next boat, so John decided to stop at a nearby tavern. Before long he was feeling no pain.

When he got back to the ferry slip, the ferryboat was just eight feet from the dock. Smith, afraid of missing this one and being late for dinner, took a running leap and landed right on the deck of the boat.

"How did you like that jump, buddy?" said a proud John to a deck hand.

"It was great," said the sailor. "But why didn't you wait? We were just pulling in!"

* * * * *

Chick went into a bar wearing such a tight pair of pants that the lounge lizard watching her asked her, "Honey, how do you get into your pants?"

She smiled and said, "You can start by ordering me a drink!"

The below are valid reasons as to why drinking should be allowed at work. If you use them wisely, you may even be able to convince your boss into allowing alcohol.

1. It's an incentive to show up.
2. It reduces stress.
3. It leads to more honest communications.
4. It reduces complaints about low pay.
5. It cuts down on time off because you can work with a hangover.
6. Employees tell management what they think, not what management wants to hear.
7. It helps save on heating costs in the winter.
8. It encourages carpooling.
9. Increases job satisfaction because if you have a bad job you don't care.
10. It eliminates vacations because people would rather come to work.
11. It makes fellow employees look better.
12. It makes the cafeteria food taste better.
13. Bosses are more likely to hand out raises when they are wasted.
14. Salary negotiations are a lot more profitable.
15. If some one does something stupid on the job, it will be quickly forgotten.

One night, this guy come into a bar and asks the bartender for a drink. Then he asks for another. After a couple more drinks, the bartender gets worried.

"What's the matter?" the bartender asks.

"My wife and I got into a fight," explained the guy, "and now she hasn't talked to me for a whole thirty-one days."

The bartender thought about this for a while. "But, isn't it a good thing that she isn't talking to you?" asked the bartender.

"Yeah, except today is the last night."

* * * * *

A golf club walks into a local bar and asks the barman for a pint of beer.

The barman refuses to serve him. "Why not," asks the golf club.

"You'll be driving later," replies the bartender.

John and Jessica were on their way home from the bar one night and John got pulled over by the police. The officer told John that he was stopped because his tail light was burned out. John said, "I'm very sorry officer, I didn't realise it was out, I'll get it fixed right away."

Just then Jessica said, "I knew this would happen when I told you two days ago to get that light fixed."

So the officer asked for John's license and after looking at it said, "Sir your license has expired."

And again John apologized and mentioned that he didn't realise that it had expired and would take care of it first thing in the morning.

Jessica said, "I told you a week ago that the state sent you a letter telling you that your license had expired."

Well by this time, John is a bit upset with his wife contradicting him in front of the officer, and he said in a rather loud voice, "Jessica, will you shut up!"

The officer then leaned over toward Jessica and asked. "Does your husband always talk to you like that?"

Jessica replied, "Only when he's drunk."

A man walks into a bar, and as he makes his way to the counter, he stops and talks to everyone in the bar. As he finishes with each group of people, they all get up and leave and go stand outside the window, looking in. Finally, the bar is empty except for this guy and the bartender. The man walks up to the counter, and says to the bartender, "I bet you $1,000 that I can spray beer from my mouth into a shot glass from thirty feet away, and not get any outside the glass."

The bartender thinks that this guy is a nutcase, but he wants his $1,000, so he agrees. The bartender gets out a shot glass, paces off thirty feet, and the contest begins. The man sprays beer all over the bar. He doesn't even touch the shot glass. When he finishes, the bartender looks at him and says, "Well, I guess you owe me $1,000, huh?"

The man answers, "Yeah, but I bet all of those people outside the window $500 a piece that I could come in here and spray beer all over the bar."

Two guys were in a bar, and they were both watching the television when the news came on. It showed a guy on a bridge who was about to jump, obviously suicidal. "I'll bet you $10 he'll jump," said the first guy.

"Bet you $10 he won't," said the second guy.

Then, the guy on the television closed his eyes and threw himself off the bridge. The second guy hands the first guy the money.

"I can't take your money," said the first guy. "I cheated you. The same story was on the five o'clock news."

"No, no. Take it," said the second guy. "I saw the five o'clock news too. I just didn't think the guy was dumb enough to jump again!"

* * * * *

How does a man show he's planning for the future?

He buys two cases of beer instead of one.

A seaman meets a pirate in a bar, and take turns boasting of their adventures on the high seas. The seaman notes that the pirate has a peg-leg, hook, and an eyepatch.

The seaman asks "So, how did you end up with the peg-leg?"

The pirate replies "We were in a storm at sea, and I was swept overboard into a school of sharks. Just as my men were pulling me out a shark bit my leg off."

"Wow!" said the seaman. "What about your hook"?

"Well...," replied the pirate, "While my men and I were plundering in the middle east, I was caught stealing from a merchant and the punishment for theft in the middle east is the loss of the hand that steals."

"Incredible!" remarked the seaman. "How did you get the eyepatch?"

"A sea gull dropping fell into my eye," replied the pirate.

"You lost your eye to a sea gull dropping?" the sailor asked incredulously.

"Well...," said the pirate, "it was my first day with the hook."

A man walks into a bar and the bartender says, "I'm sorry, I can't serve you here unless you are wearing a tie."

The man says, "Okay, I'll be right back," and goes to his car to find anything he can use for a tie. All he finds is a set of jumper cables, so he ties them around his neck, goes back in and asks, "How's this?"

The bartender replies, "Well, okay, but don't start anything."

* * * * *

A big hulking hooligan walks into a bar, slams his fist down, and yells, "Give me a Budweiser, or...!" Scared, the bartender serves the man his Budweiser. This happens everyday for a week straight, and the bartender turns into a nervous wreck. He asks his wife for advice, and she tells him he should stand up for himself. Easier said than done, he thinks, but he decides to try it. The next day, the hooligan returns.

"Give me a Budweiser, or...!"

"O-o-o-o-r-r-r w-what?" stammers the bartender.

"A small Coke."

A good Samaritan was walking home late one night when he came upon this drunk on the sidewalk. Wanting to help, he asked the drunk, "do you live here?"

"Yep."

"Would you like me to help you upstairs?"

"Yep."

When they got up on the second floor, the good person asked "Is this your floor?"

"Yep."

Then the good Samaritan got to thinking that maybe he didn't want to face the man's irate and tired wife because she may think he was the one who got the man drunk. So, he opened the first door he came to and shoved him through it then went back downstairs. However, when he went back outside, there was another drunk. So he asked that drunk, "Do you live here?"

"Yep".

"Would you like me to help you upstairs?"

"Yep".

So he did and put him in the same door with the first drunk. Then went back downstairs.

Where, to his surprise, there was another drunk. So he started over to him. But before he got to him, the drunk staggered over to a policeman and cried, "Please officer, protect me from this man. He's been doing nothing all night long but taking me upstairs and throwing me down the elevator shaft!"

* * * * *

A preacher goes into a bar and says, "Anybody who wants to go to heaven, stand up."

Everybody stands up except for a drunk in the corner.

The preacher says, "My son, don't you want to go to heaven when you die?"

The drunk says, "When I die? Sure. I thought you were taking a load up now."

* * * * *

A cop pulls over a drunk driver. The drunk driver says, "Ossssifer, you need to get your records straight. You just asked me for my license, but you took it away yesterday!"

One day, after striking gold in Alaska, a lonesome miner came down from the mountains and walked into a saloon in the nearest town. "I'm lookin' for the meanest, roughest and toughest whore in the Yukon!" he said to the bartender.

"Well, we got her!" replied the barkeep. "She's upstairs in the second room on the right." The miner handed the bartender a gold nugget to pay for the whore and two beers.

He grabbed the bottles, stomped up the stairs, kicked open the second door on the right and yelled, "I'm lookin' for the meanest, roughest and toughest whore in the Yukon!"

The woman inside the room looked at the miner and said, "You found her!" Then she stripped naked, bent over and grabbed her ankles.

"How do you know I want to do it in that position?" asked the miner.

"I don't," replied the whore, "but I thought you might like to open those beers first."

The local bar was so sure that its bartender was the strongest man around they had a standing $1000 bet. The bartender would squeeze a lemon until all the juice ran into a glass, and hand the lemon to a patron. Anyone who could squeeze one more drop of juice out would win the money. Many people had tried over time but nobody could do it. One day, a scrawny little man came in, wearing thick glasses and a polyester suit.

"I'd like to try the bet," he said in a tiny, squeaky voice. After the laughter had died down, the bartender grabbed a lemon, and squeezed away. He handed the wrinkled remains of the rind to the little man. But the crowd's laughter turned to total silence as the man clenched his fist around the lemon and six drops fell into the glass. As the crowd cheered, the bartender paid the $1000 and asked the little man what he did for a living. Was he a lumberjack, or a weightlifter, or what?

"I'm a tax man!"

A guy walks into a bar with a small dog. The bartender says, "Get out of here with that dog!"

The guy says, "But this isn't just any dog... this dog can play the piano!"

The bartender replies, "Well, if he can play that piano, you both can stay, and have a drink on the house!"

So the guy sits the dog on the piano stool, and the dog starts playing. Ragtime, Mozart, and the bartender and patrons are enjoying the music.

Suddenly a bigger dog runs in, grabs the small dog by the scruff of the neck, and drags him out. The bartender asks the guy, "What was that all about?"

The guy replies, "Oh, that was his mother. She wanted him to be a doctor."

* * * * *

Two peanuts walk into a pub and one was assaulted.

This white guy walks into a bar and he starts talking with a black guy who is sitting next to him. After a couple of beers they decide to go take a pee together. As they are in the men's room, the white guy glances at the black's dick.

"Gee, I really wish I had a dick like that," says the white guy.

"Well," says the black, "All you have to do is hit your penis on the bath tab for ten minutes every morning, and you'll get it."

The other guy thanks him for his advice and walks out of the bar.

Some months later they meet again in the same bar, and they start talking.

"Well," says the black man, "did you take the advice?"

"I did," says the other guy.

"So, let me see."

The white guy lowers his pants and shows him his penis.

"Ha!" says the black guy, "At least you made the color like mine!"

There were three pigs.

The first pig went to a bar ordered a drink and gulped it down and went to the bathroom and then left.

The second pig went to the same bar ordered a drink and gulped it down and went to the bathroom and then left.

The third pig went to the same bar ordered a drink and gulped it down and was just going to leave and the bartender asked if he was going to the bathroom and the third little pig said, "No I'm the little pig that goes weee weee weee all the way home"

* * * * *

The drunk rang Dublin airport and inquired: 'How long does it take to fly to New York from Dublin?'

'Just a second,' said the receptionist.

'Thank you,' said the drunk and replaced the phone.

A woman is sitting at a bar, enjoying an after work cocktail with her girlfriends, when an exceptionally tall, handsome, sexy young man entered. He was so striking that the woman could not take her eyes off him. The young man noticed her overly-attentive stare and walked directly toward her. Before she could offer her apologies for being rude and staring, the young man said to her, "I'll do anything, absolutely anything, that you want me to so, no matter how kinky, for $100, on one condition." Flabbergasted, the woman asked what the condition was. The young man replied, "You have to tell me what you want me to do in just three words."

The woman considered his proposition for a moment, withdrew from her purse five $20 bills, which she slowly counted into the young man's outstretched hand. She looked deeply into his eyes and slowly, meaningfully said "Clean my house."

* * * * *

A guy walks into a bar and says "I'm so thirsty, I could lick the sweat off a bull's balls."

A gay guy in the corner goes, "MOOOOOOO!"

Two blokes go into a pub.

Fred says to Jeff, "Right Donkey, two pints then, a pint of Guiness for me and what is it you want Donkey?"

Jeff: "A puh phuh puh p-p-pint of Guh Guh Guh Guh Guineeessssss, a puh phu phu pint of Guh Guiness"

Fred: "Ok, bartender—two pints of Guiness please, one for me and one for Donkey"

So they sit with their guiness and drink away. Fred finishes first and gets up,"Right Donkey, I'm going for a piss, get the next round in will you Donkey? Thanks Donkey."

Jeff gets up and goes to the bar—"Two puh puh puh puh pints of Guh Guh Guh Guh Guh Guiness puh puh puh please."

The bartender says "Certainly"

While he pours the pints he says to Jeff,"I think it's disgusting how he keeps calling you Donkey all the time"

Jeff looks at the bartender and says, "Oh, hee-aw, hee-aw, hee-aw, hee-always calls me that!

A Panda walks into a bar and asks the bartender for a meal. When the meal finally arrives, he eats it quickly, then shoots a drunk, and leaves the bar.

A patron walks over to the bartender and asks, "What was that all about?"

The bartender replies, "Look up 'panda' in the dictionary, pal."

And so, the patron retrieves his Webster's dictionary from his coat pocket and looks up the word 'panda.'

"What's it say?" asks the bartender.

The patron replies with a grin, "Eats shoots and leaves."

* * * * *

Two cartons of yogurt walk into a bar. The bartender, a tub of cottage cheese, says to them, "We don't serve your kind in here." One of the yogurt cartons says back to him, "Why not? We're cultured individuals."

A circus owner walked into a bar to see everyone crowded about a table watching a little show. On the table was an upside down pot and a duck tap dancing on it. The circus owner was so impressed that he offered to buy the duck from its owner. After some wheeling and dealing, they settled for $10,000 for the duck and the pot.

Three days later the circus owner runs back to the bar in anger, "Your duck is a ripoff! I put him on the pot before a whole audience, and he didn't dance a single step!"

"So?" asked the ducks former owner, "did you remember to light the candle under the pot?"

* * * * *

A seal walks into a bar and asks the bartender for a drink.

The bartender asks the seal, "What's your pleasure?"

The seal replies, "Anything but Canadian Club."

A man had been out in the back woods for weeks, cutting logs. He was a bit scruffy and didn't smell very good. Finally he needed a break and came in to town for a few beers.

In the bar, he saw the local jock of the town's football team. He was bragging about his girlfriend and how she was lucky to have him for a boyfriend.

The lumberjack, after drinking six bottles of beer, was heard to say, "Buddy, if she went out with me, she'd never go out with you ever again."

To which the local jock replied, "Hey buddy, if she went out with you, she'd never go out with ANYONE ever again."

* * * * *

A regular at Bob's Bar came in one evening sporting a matched pair of swollen black eyes that appeared extremely painful.

"Whoa, Sam!" said the bartender. "Who gave those beauties to you?"

"Nobody gave them to me," said Sam. "I had to fight like crazy for both of them."

One day, three friends went to this "Gentlemen's Club." One of the friends wanted to impress the other two, so he pulls out a $10 bill. The "dancer" came over to them, and the one friend licked the $10 and put it on her butt.

Not to be outdone, the other friend pulls out a $50 bill. He calls the girl back over, licks the $50, and puts it on her other cheek.

Now the attention is focused on the third guy. He got out his wallet, thought for a minute, then got out his ATM card, swiped it down her crack, grabbed the $60, and headed for the door.

* * * * *

A farmer in one small Welsh village was regarded with some disfavour by the local chapel-goers because both he and his wife were heavy drinkers and indeed were known to drink beer out of the teapot.

However, they were induced to attend a frenzied revival meeting in the chapel and were so affected by this that both of them gave up their intemperate habits.

At the next meeting the farmer came forward to testify to the change in his life.

"Yes," he declared, "the Lord has converted me, has converted my wife and has converted the teapot."

Yesterday, scientists in the United States revealed that beer contains small traces of female hormones.

To prove their theory, they fed one hundred men twelve pints of beer and observed that 100% of them started talking nonsense and couldn't drive.

* * * * *

So this new bar opens and the owner can't think of a name. So he decides to name the bar after the third person who walks in. It takes dosen't take long and soon the third customer walks in.

The owner jumps up and walks over to the girl. "You're the third person to enter my bar and I'm going to name it after you."

"Okay," she says, "My name is Jill."

The owner looks her over and says, "I like your legs so I'm going to name the bar 'Jill's Legs'"

The next day a bum is sitting outside the bar and a cop askes him what he's doing. He answers, "Waiting for Jill's Legs to open so I can get a drink!"

A very sexy redhead walks into a pub and takes a seat at the end of the bar.

The bartender says to her, "What can I get ya?"

The woman replies, "Give me a Busch Beer."

The bartender gets the beer and sets it in front of her. The woman immediately picks up the beer, slams it down and passes out cold. Three men from the bar drag her out back and have their way with her.

The following night, the same woman goes back to the same pub, takes a seat at the same place at the end of the bar, and the same bartender asks, "What can I get ya?"

The woman replies, "Give me a Busch Beer."

The bartender gets the beer and sets it in front of her. The woman immediately picks up the beer, slams it down and passes out cold. Four men from the bar drag her out back and have their way with her.

The following night, the same woman goes back to the same pub, takes a seat at the same place at the end of the bar, and the same bartender says, "I know, you want a Busch..."

The woman stops him and says, "No, you better make it a Bud Light, that Busch makes my pussy hurt."

A man walks in a bar and a little man is sitting next to him. The little man asked if he had a family and how old he was. The man told him he was 29 and had a wife and two kids.

The little man says, "I'm a Leprechaun, and if you let me F#$@ you in the butt I will grant you three wishes."

They go to the bathroom and the Leprechaun starts to F@$# him in the butt.

When almost finished the Leprechaun says, "You did say you had a family right?"

Than man replies, "Yes I'm 29 and have a wife and two kids."

The Leprechaun says, "Well aren't you a little bit old to be believing in Leprechauns?"

* * * * *

A woman at a party walked up to a man and told him, "If you were my husband I would poison your drink."

The man replied, "If you were my wife I would drink it."

A guy walks into a pub and sees a sign hanging over the bar which reads:

Cheese Sandwich: $1.50
Chicken Sandwich: $2.50
Hand Job: $5.00

Checking his wallet for the necessary payment, he walks up to the bar and beckons to one of the three exceptionally attractive blondes serving drinks to an eager-looking group of men.

"Yes?" she enquires with a knowing smile, "Can I help you?"

"I was wondering", whispers the man, "are you the one who gives the hand-jobs?"

"Yes," she purrs, "I am."

The man replies, "Well wash your f@$#ing hands, I want a cheese sandwich!"

THINGS THAT ARE DIFFICULT TO SAY WHEN YOU'RE DRUNK:
Indubitably
Innovative
Preliminary
Cinnamon

THINGS THAT ARE VERY DIFFICULT TO SAY WHEN YOU'RE DRUNK:
Specificity
British
Constitution
Passive-aggressive disorder
Loquacious
Transubstantiate

THINGS THAT ARE DOWNRIGHT IMPOSSIBLE TO SAY WHEN YOU'RE DRUNK:
Thanks, but I don't want to have sex.
Nope, no more booze for me.
Sorry, but you're not really my type.
Good evening officer, isn't it lovely out tonight.
Oh, I just couldn't. No one wants to hear me sing.

A man had been drinking at the bar for hours when he mentioned something about his girlfriend being out in the car.

The bartender, concerned because it was so cold, went to check on her.

When he looked inside the car, he saw the drunk's buddy, Pete, and his girlfriend going at it in the back seat.

The bartender shook his head and walked back inside. He told the drunk that he thought it might be a good idea to check on his girlfriend.

The drunk staggered outside to the car, saw Pete and his girlfriend entwined, then walked back into the bar laughing.

"What's so funny?" the bartender asked.

"That damned Pete!" the drunk chortled, "He's so drunk, he thinks he's me!"

* * * * *

Q: What to do if beer interferes with the job?

A: Get off the job.

A truck driver, hauling a tractor-trailer load of computers, stops for a beer. As he approaches the bar, he sees a big sign on the door that says, "COMPUTER NERDS NOT ALLOWED—ENTER AT YOUR OWN RISK!" He enters and sits down.

The bartender comes over to him, sniffs, and says that he smells kind of nerdy. He then asks him what he does for a living. The truck driver explains to him that he drives a truck, and the smell is just from the computers he is hauling. The bartender serves him a beer and says, "Okay, truck drivers aren't nerds."

As he is sipping his beer, a skinny guy walks in wearing a pair of glasses with tape around the middle, a pocket protector with twelve kinds of pens and pencils, and a belt that is at least a foot too long. The bartender, without saying a word, pulls out a shotgun and blows the guy away. The truck driver asks him why he did that.

The bartender replied, "Don't worry. The computer nerds are in season because they are over-populating Silicon Valley. You don't even need a license."

So the truck driver finishes his beer, gets back in his truck, and heads for the freeway. Suddenly, he veers to avoid an accident, and the load shifts. The back door breaks open and computers spill out all over the road. He jumps out and sees a crowd already forming, snatching up all of the computers. The scavengers are comprised of engineers, accountants and programmers—computer geeks. Each of them wearing the nerdiest clothes he has ever seen.

He can't let them steal his whole load. So remembering what happened in the bar, he pulls out his gun and starts blasting away, killing several of them instantly. A highway patrol officer comes zooming up and jumps out of the car screaming at him to stop.

The truck driver said, "What's wrong? I thought computer nerds were in season."

"Well, sure," says the patrolman, "But you can't bait 'em!"

* * * * *

A man walked into a bar, leading an alligator by a leash. He asked the bartender, "Do you serve lawyers here?"
"Sure do," said the bartender.
"Good," replied the man. "Give me a beer, and I'll have a lawyer for my 'gator'".

While the bar patron savored a double martini, an attractive women sat down next to him. The bartender served her a glass of orange juice, and the man turned to her and said, "This is a special day. I'm celebrating."

"I'm celebrating, too," she replied, clinking glasses with him.

"What are you celebrating?" he asked.

"For years I've been trying to have a child," she answered, "Today my gynecologist told me I'm pregnant!"

"Congratulations," the man said, lifting his glass.

"As it happens, I'm a chicken farmer, and for years all my hens were infertile. But today they're finally fertile."

"How did it happen?"

"I switched cocks."

"What a coincidence," she said, smiling.

* * * * *

At 3.00 am a desk clerk at a hotel gets a call from a drunk guy asking what time the bar opens. "It opens at noon," answers the clerk.

About an hour later he gets a call from the same guy, sounding even drunker. "What time does the bar open?" he asks.

"Same time as before... Noon!" Replies the clerk.

Another hour passes and he calls again, plastered, "Whatjoo shay the bar opins at?"

The clerk then answers, "It opens at noon, but if you can't wait, I can have room service send something up to you."

"No... I don't wanna git in... Ah wanna git OUT!"

* * * * *

A drunk is taking a leak right on the street. A policeman says to him: "You could have done it behind the corner!"

"My dick is no fire hose, you know?"

A drunk staggers into a diner and orders a couple of eggs. The waiter, suspecting that they've run out, goes back to question the chef, "Hey, Gus, do we have any more eggs?"

Gus replies, "I ran out of fresh eggs, I only have two rotten eggs left."

The waiter says, "Give him the rotten eggs. He's so bombed he won't know the difference."

Gus scrambles up the rotten eggs and heaps on hash browns, sausage and toast. The drunk is so hungry he wolfs down the breakfast without comment. He goes to pay the cashier and asks, "Where'd you get those eggs?"

She replies, "We have our own chicken farm."

The drunk asks, "Do you have a rooster?

"No," she says.

The drunk replies, "Well, you'd better get one, because some skunk is screwing your chickens."

Two construction workers were sitting in a bar one day, drinking a few beers. The bartender noticed that they were intent on something on their table, but couldn't see what it was. Suddenly, both men jumped up, high-fived each other, and shouted, "Fifty-five!"

Curious, the bartender went over to see what they were doing. "Did somebody win a bet?" he asked.

One of the construction workers replied, "No, but we stopped at Toys R Us on the way over and got a puzzle. It says right on the box '2 to 4 years,' but we got it done in fifty-five minutes!"

* * * * *

The young son of some English immigrants got tired of his mates ragging him about being a pom, so he asked them how he could become a fair-dinkum Aussie. They told him that he would have to go to the pub, order up a meat pie and a beer and in the presence of two witnesses, eat the pie and drink the beer. After that he'd be a true-blue Australian.

That evening, after school, he stopped off at the local pub and ordered the pie and a beer. The publican said he'd sell him the pie, but he was way too young for a beer. At this, the boy became visibly upset, so the publican's wife asked him what was wrong and he told her. After an exchange of glances, the couple took the boy into the office and witnessed his initiation as an Aussie.

When he arrived home late, his mum wanted to know where he'd been, so he told her. "Down at the pub, having a meat pie and a beer." This reply earned him a cuff on the ear and a warning that his Dad would be home soon and he'd better not lie to him. When the boy's father came home, he asked the same question and received the same answer. "Down at the pub, having a meat pie and a beer."

His father gave him a couple of belts on the bum and sent him to his room. As he turned to leave, the boy said, "I know what it's like to be an Australian. I've only been an Aussie for a couple of hours and I'm already starting to hate you bloody poms!"

One night, a police officer was staking out a particularly rowdy bar for possible violations of the driving-under-the-influence laws. At closing time, he saw a fellow stumble out of the bar, trip on the curb, and try his keys on five different cars before he found his. Then, sat in the front seat fumbling around with his keys for several minutes. Everyone else left the bar and drove off. Finally, the fellow started his engine and began to pull away. The police officer was waiting for him. He stopped the driver, read him his rights and administered the Breathalyzer test. The results showed a reading of 0.0. The puzzled officer demanded to know how that could be.

The driver replied, "Tonight, I'm the designated decoy"

* * * * *

A female police officer arrests a guy for drunk driving.

While reading him his Rights, the female officer tells the man: "Sir, you have the right to remain silent. Anything you say, can and will be held against you."

"Boobs," the drunk replied.

* * * * *